COMMERCIAL TRANSACTIONS HANDBOOK

2002 Cumulative Supplement

COMMERCIAL REAL ESTATE TRANSACTIONS HANDBOOK
THIRD EDITION

2002 Cumulative Supplement

MARK A. SENN
Editor

ASPEN LAW & BUSINESS
A Division of Aspen Publishers, Inc.
New York   Gaithersburg

This publication is designed to provide accurate and authoritative information in regard to the subject matter covered. It is sold with the understanding that the publisher is not engaged in rendering legal, accounting, or other professional services. If legal advice or other professional assistance is required, the services of a competent professional person should be sought.

—From a *Declaration of Principles* jointly adopted by a Committee of the American Bar Association and a Committee of Publishers and Associations

Copyright © 2002 by Aspen Law & Business
A Division of Aspen Publishers, Inc.
A Wolters Kluwer Company
www.aspenpublishers.com

All rights reserved. No part of this publication may be reproduced or transmitted in any form or by any means, electronic or mechanical, including photocopy, recording, or any information storage and retrieval system, without permission in writing from the publisher. Requests for permission to make copies of any part of this publication should be mailed to:

Permissions
Aspen Law & Business
1185 Avenue of the Americas
New York, NY 10036

Printed in the United States of America

1 2 3 4 5 6 7 8 9 0

Library of Congress Cataloging-in-Publication Data

Commercial real estate transactions handbook / [edited by] Mark Senn.—3rd ed.
    p. cm.
  Rev. ed. of: Negotiating and structuring real estate transactions. 2nd ed. c1993.
  Includes index.
  ISBN 0-7355-0573-X
  ISBN 0-7355-2989-2 (supplement)
    1. Vendors and purchasers—United States. 2. Real estate development—Law and legislation United States. 3. Mortgages—United States. 4. Commercial leases—United States. I. Senn, Mark A. II. Negotiating and structuring real estate transactions.

KF665 .C575 2000
346.7304'37 dc21   00-038037

About Aspen Law & Business

Aspen Law & Business is a leading publisher of authoritative treatises, practice manuals, services, and journals for attorneys, corporate and bank directors, accountants, auditors, environmental compliance professionals, financial and tax advisors, and other business professionals. Our mission is to provide practical solution-based how-to information keyed to the latest original pronouncements, as well as the latest legislative, judicial, and regulatory developments.

We offer publications in the areas of accounting and auditing; antitrust; banking and finance; bankruptcy; business and commercial law; construction law; corporate law; criminal law; environmental compliance; government and administrative law; health law; insurance law; intellectual property; international law; legal practice and litigation; matrimonial and family law; pensions, benefits, and labor; real estate law; securities; and taxation.

Other Aspen Law & Business products treating real estate law issues include:

Commercial Real Estate Leases: Preparation, Negotiation, and Forms (Third Edition)
Environmental Liability and Real Property Transactions: Law and Practice (Second Edition)
Handbook of Massachusetts Land Use and Planning Law
Law of Property Rights Protection: Limitations on Governmental Powers
Law of Real Estate Brokers
Law of Title Insurance
Managing and Leasing Commercial Properties: Practice, Strategies, and Forms (Third Edition)

ASPEN LAW & BUSINESS
A Division of Aspen Publishers, Inc.
A Wolters Kluwer Company
www.aspenpublishers.com

SUBSCRIPTION NOTICE

This Aspen Law & Business product is updated on a periodic basis with supplements to reflect important changes in the subject matter. If you purchased this product directly from Aspen Law & Business, we have already recorded your subscription for the update service.

If, however, you purchased this product from a bookstore and wish to receive future updates and revised or related volumes billed separately with a 30-day examination review, please contact our Customer Service Department at 1-800-234-1660, or send your name, company name (if applicable), address, and the title of the product to:

ASPEN LAW & BUSINESS
A Division of Aspen Publishers, Inc.
7201 McKinney Circle
Frederick, MD 21704

CONTENTS

Sections listed below appear only in the supplement and not in the main volume.

Chapter 4
CONSTRUCTION CONTRACTS 1

§ 4.09 The Design/Build Movement.. 1
    [A] Growth of Design/Build 1
    [B] History of Design/Build 2
    [C] Advantages of Design/Build................................... 2
    [D] Disadvantages of Design/Build 3
    [E] Selecting the Right Project Delivery System 4
    [F] Ramifications of Selection for Roles, Relationships, Rights, and Responsibilities... 5
    [G] Making Design/Build Work.................................... 6

Chapter 8
NEGOTIATING LOAN TRANSACTIONS 9

§ 8.03 Loan Documents 10
    [B] Promissory Note 10
        [4] "Lock In" and Prepayment Penalty Clauses................ 11

Chapter 9
OPINION LETTERS IN REAL ESTATE LOAN TRANSACTIONS 17
    Appendix 9C Sample Legal Opinion.. 19

Chapter 10
BASIC RISK ALLOCATION AND INSURANCE CONCEPTS FOR REAL ESTATE TRANSACTIONS.. 41
    Appendix 10G Deed of Trust Insurance, Indemnity, and Waiver Provisions (Mortgagee's Form).............................. 43

Chapter 11
ENVIRONMENTAL ISSUES IN COMMERCIAL REAL ESTATE SALES AND LEASES 51

§ 11.12 Environmental Risk Insurance 58
  [A] Types of Coverage 59
  [B] Pollution Legal Liability Insurance 60
  [C] Cost Overrun Insurance 61
  [D] Brownfield Insurance 62
  [E] Secured Creditor Insurance 63
  [F] Policy Exclusions 64

Chapter 12
INDUSTRIAL LEASES 67

§ 12.15 Condemnation and Casualty Provisions That Shift Risk to the Tenant 67

Chapter 14
OFFICE LEASES 73

Chapter 16
COMMON INTEREST OWNERSHIP 77

Chapter 17
BANKRUPTCY 83

Index *89*

CHAPTER 4
CONSTRUCTION CONTRACTS
Philip E. Beck

§ 4.02 CONTRACT STRUCTURE: CHOOSING A CONTRACTUAL RELATIONSHIP

[E] Design/Build

Page 147, add at end of subsection [E]:

Due to its increasing popularity in recent years, and projections by construction industry insiders that this trend will continue in the decade ahead, design/build is discussed in greater detail in §§ **4.09[A]** through **[G]** of this supplement.

Page 205, add new section:

§ 4.09 THE DESIGN/BUILD MOVEMENT

[A] Growth of Design/Build

In § **4.02[E]** of the main volume, design/build construction was introduced as one of the four common construction contracting structures, or "project delivery systems." "Design/build," as that phrase is used in the construction industry, denotes the situation in which the owner of a project contracts with a single entity to both design the project and construct the project in accordance with that design. Thus, the owner who selects this project delivery system needs to look only to a single source for both design and construction.

The design/builder may be a company possessing both design and construction capabilities in-house; it may be a general contractor who, in turn, hires an architect/engineer to design the project, operating essentially as a subcontractor to the design/builder; it may, in some states,[128] be an architect/engineer who, in turn, hires a contractor to construct its design; or it may be a joint venture (a partnership formed for the limited purpose of performing a specific project) comprised of one or more design firms plus one or more construction firms.

Use of the design/build project delivery system has increased exponentially over the past two decades, with design/build quickly becoming the project delivery system of choice in the United States and throughout the world. Estimates indicate that by the mid-1990s design/build accounted for ten times the construction volume it accounted for just 10 years earlier. Many predict that by 2010 design/build will account for 50 percent of the nonresidential construction market in the United States. Perhaps more impressive, design/build is rapidly becoming the preferred method of project delivery in the public sector, as well as the private sector. This is true despite the fact that competitive bidding laws in many states had to be rewritten before many public owners could utilize design/build.[129]

[B] History of Design/Build

Like many "new" ideas, design/build is actually the rebirth of an old one. The modern-day design/builders closely resemble the "master builders" of yesteryear, who built the wondrous pyramids of Egypt, the Great Wall of China, and India's Taj Mahal. Obviously, construction techniques have changed a great deal since those ancient projects were constructed, and most modern-day construction projects do not take hundreds of years to complete. Yet the underlying philosophy that it is better to simplify the contract structure by having a single point of responsibility and accountability for both design and construction is as sound today as it was then. Thus, the use of the design/build project delivery approach, for appropriate projects, truly does reflect "the wisdom of the ages."

Moreover, advocates of design/build argue that the inherent benefits of design/build are even more relevant today than they were in the days of old. The modern-day construction process involves legal, regulatory, environmental, societal, technological, economic, financial, market-related, timing, and other challenges and constraints that the master builders of yore could not have even imagined. Out of this greater complexity comes an even greater need to simplify the process by unifying responsibilities.

[C] Advantages of Design/Build

The remarkable growth in the popularity of design/build in recent years is evidence of the fact that owners of construction projects perceive its advantages to outweigh its disadvantages, at least for many projects. Some of the major advantages of design/build include:

1. The single point of design and construction responsibility characteristic of design/build shifts the risks of design deficiencies and conflicts between the designer and the contractor from the owner to the design/builder, resulting in less project risk for the owner.

2. Design/build tends to produce a shorter "time to market" and to better facilitate "fast track" construction (i.e., construction that proceeds as design work is still being performed). Studies have suggested that design/build projects are approximately one-third faster than traditional "design—then bid—then build" projects and approximately one-fourth faster than projects utilizing a "construction manager at-risk" (a construction manager with schedule and budget responsibility). In today's world, such time savings can be of critical importance.

3. Design/build tends to provide greater predictability and control of both the project schedule and the project budget, due to the consolidation of design and construction responsibility and accountability.

4. Design/build allows both the contractor and the designer to be actively involved in the project from the very early stages, providing the owner the benefit of both disciplines' input in the early project planning and design.

5. Design/build tends to promote greater cooperation, coordination, and teamwork between the contractor and the designer, and within the entire project team, and to result in less "finger pointing" between the contractor and the designer.

6. Design/build typically reduces the owner's administrative burden and produces less frustration and aggravation for the owner.

7. Design/build usually breeds fewer claims, disputes, and lawsuits than other project delivery systems.

[D] Disadvantages of Design/Build

Like everything in life, design/build involves certain trade-offs. Some of the major disadvantages of design/build are:

1. With the lower risk that is characteristic of design/build may come less control and less reward, as more decisions are left to the discretion of the design/builder.

2. The consolidation of design and construction responsibility under a single entity removes the "checks and balances" system that exists when the designer and the contractor are separate, autonomous entities, both working for the owner. This factor alone causes some owners to reject design/build for fear that "the fox would be guarding the hen house" and that problems would be "swept under the rug."
3. The contractor selection process is both costly and time-consuming with design/build.
4. For public owners particularly, design/build procurement may be difficult or complicated, or it may not be legally permissible.
5. By vesting more power and responsibility in the design/builder, some feel the owner has less quality assurance and quality control.130
6. Under design/build, the owner relinquishes some of its control and flexibility in developing the design of the project. If an owner wishes to micro-manage the design process and make continuous changes to the design, the promise of greater budget control and schedule control becomes illusory.
7. Because it is still new to some, participants in the design/build process sometimes do not fully understand their roles and responsibilities, which can lead to problems. In addition, the insurance policies carried by many design and construction firms, as well as state licensing laws, may not be compatible with the characteristics of design/build.

[E] Selecting the Right Project Delivery System

An owner should consider a number of factors in deciding which of the available project delivery systems is best suited to that owner and the particular project involved. Design/build works better for some owners and some types of projects than for others. Some of the factors an owner should consider when selecting a project delivery system include:

1. Are there legal or political requirements or considerations (such as public procurement laws and state licensing laws)?
2. How critical is the project schedule?
3. How critical is the project budget?
4. How well defined are the owner's needs?
5. How complex is the project?

6. What are the capabilities, sophistication, and experience of each of the parties?
7. How much control does the owner desire/can the owner handle?
8. How much do the parties trust one another?

Both logic and experience suggest that design/build is best suited for certain types of projects. Among these are projects in which the owner's needs and requirements are clearly defined at the outset, projects involving the repetition of prior design and construction (such as fast-food chain restaurants), projects in which less owner input is desired and required, projects driven by performance needs rather than aesthetics (such as manufacturing facilities), projects in which "time to market" is critical (such as a manufacturing plant required to bring a new product to market quickly), and projects for owners who are particularly risk-averse.

[F] Ramifications of Selection for Roles, Relationships, Rights, and Responsibilities

Regardless of whether the project delivery system chosen for a particular project is design/build or one of the other alternatives, it is imperative to the success of a project that the project participants fully understand their respective roles, the relationships of their roles to one another, and their respective rights and responsibilities. Each contract structure carries with it a unique set of party roles and relationships and creates a unique set of rights and responsibilities. In order to assess and manage the risks inherent in every construction project, the parties should make sure they know, and agree upon, who is responsible, and to what extent, for each of the following:

1. Suitability of the design;
2. Design changes;
3. Coordination of contractors;
4. Control of the schedule;
5. Control of the budget;
6. Unforeseen subsurface conditions;
7. Changes in market conditions;
8. Any loss of productivity;

9. Unanticipated schedule impacts; and

10. The unexpected.

Owners, contractors, and designers who are new to design/build are sometimes surprised at some of their responsibilities. For example, contractors are not accustomed to being accountable to the owner for the suitability of the project design, as they are under design/build. This is the complete opposite of the *Spearin* doctrine, discussed in § **4.03[C][1]**, at pages 151–153 of the main volume. Contractors also typically assume far greater risks with respect to unanticipated subsurface site conditions under design/build construction than with other project delivery systems.

[G] Making Design/Build Work

As with any construction project, the biggest key to a successful design/build project is to select the right project team. If an owner is fortunate enough to select a good design/builder who is experienced in projects of the type involved, possesses the requisite expertise, is dedicated to working as a member of the team to make the project a success, and will dedicate the right mix of capable personnel and company resources to the project, the project is well on its way to being a success. While the selection of the best contract structure for a particular project is important, the selection of the right people to fill in the boxes on the organizational chart is even more so. This may be even more critical under the design/build project delivery approach than under other contracting structures.

Part of the trick to selecting the right project participants is implementing an appropriate selection process. Selection of a design/builder generally should be a two-step process consisting of a prequalification phase, during which the initial list of candidates is reduced to a "short list," and a final selection phase, during which the design/builder for the project is selected from the design/builders who made the short list. As noted previously, the selection process for a design/build project can be very costly, complicated, and time-consuming. It is imperative, however, that the owner use a reasonable, but thorough, selection process. To avoid any unnecessary costs, the owner should generally require minimal design documentation to be submitted during the prequalification phase, focusing more on the qualifications of the candidates and their compatibility with the owner and the project. The owner should also seriously consider paying each of the unsuccessful candidates who made the short list a stipend to help defray the costs necessarily incurred in pursuing the project and to partially compensate them for their contributions to the project.

Once the design/builder is selected, and as part of the selection process itself, the owner should develop and implement a good design/build contract that clearly defines each party's rights and responsibilities and clearly allocates project risks. The Associated General Contractors of America has developed a good set of design/build contract forms that have been endorsed by owners, contractors, and designers alike. These can be used in lieu of a customized contract if the project budget will not support one or can be used as a starting point in preparing a contract tailored to the unique needs of a specific project.

As suggested previously, if the project is to be successful, it is important for the project participants to fully identify and understand each party's rights and responsibilities and to recognize, allocate, and manage the various risks inherent in any construction project. All of the parties must also be committed to using the design/build process, to working together as a team, and to achieving the project's objectives.

For design/build to work as intended, it is imperative that the owner provide the design/builder, at the outset, a clear statement of the owner's program requirements, with the scope and intent of the project defined in sufficient detail to avoid any miscommunication and the disputes miscommunication can cause. The owner should also implement appropriate monitoring and quality assurance procedures throughout the project to ensure that both design and construction are progressing as envisioned.

If the right project team is assembled and the right procedures are put in place and adhered to, design/build can provide an excellent vehicle for achieving a successful project.

---

[128] In some states, such as North Carolina, current laws require that the entity holding the contract with the owner be a licensed general contractor. This effectively precludes "architect-led" design/build construction in those states, requiring "contractor-led" design/build instead.

[129] Almost by definition, when multiple bidders (or offerors) are competing for a design/build project, they are submitting prices based upon somewhat different projects, i.e., each bidder's unique design. Accordingly, design/build does not lend itself to selecting a contractor based upon the traditional competitive bidding process, where price is the only determinant, because "apples to apples" comparison is not possible. Even in the public sector, the selection of a design/builder must be based, in part, on subjective factors. In many states, new public procurement legislation had to be enacted in order to allow public owners this flexibility in the contractor selection process.

[130] Advocates of design/build, however, point to studies indicating that design/build actually produces a higher-quality project.

CHAPTER 8
NEGOTIATING LOAN TRANSACTIONS

Robert A. Thompson
Brian D. Smith

§ 8.02 LOAN APPLICATION AND COMMITMENTS

[B] Refundability of Fees

[1] Application Fees

Page 479, add at end of carryover paragraph:

Increasingly, loan applications include a combination of deposits to be applied to engineering, environmental, legal, accounting/audit, and other due diligence investigation costs and a "Lender Fee" or "Application Fee," which is deemed fully earned upon acceptance of the application.

[C] Limiting Conditions to Lender's Obligations

[3] Qualifications of Lender's Right of Approval

Page 484, add to note 4:

The doctrine of good faith and fair dealing has been acknowledged in numerous cases involving "failure to cooperate in the other party's performance" (Restatement of Contracts (Second) § 205, cmt. (d)) and "abuse of a power to determine compliance or to terminate the contract" (Restatement of Contracts (Second) § 205, cmt. (e)).

§ 8.03 LOAN DOCUMENTS

[B] Promissory Note

[2] Nonrecourse and Limited Recourse Provisions

[b] Applicable State Law

Page 504, add to note 12:

See discussion in Restatement of Property (Mortgages) § 4.6, cmt. (i).

[3] Choice of Law and Forum

Page 505, add to note 13:

For a recent analysis of the enforceability of choice of law provisions in loan documents, *see, e.g.*, Preble, "Choice of Law Opinions: Making the Right Choice," Prob. & Prop. (July/Aug. 1997), at 13.

Page 505, add after subsection [3]:

[4] "Lock In" and Prepayment Penalty Clauses

Other than being adequately secured and having effective remedies upon loan default, few issues are of greater importance to a permanent lender than maintenance of its anticipated return on its funds. As opposed to construction and land development loans, where the risk to the lender dictates encouragement of the earliest possible repayment and loan fees and other payments, rather than interest, are the primary remuneration, long-term lenders consider a reliable annual yield on investment to be crucial. The primary mechanisms for assuring this objective are "lock-in" clauses and prepayment penalties. The former is nothing more than a prohibition of prepayment for the term of the loan or some shorter specified period; the latter is a provision specifying an amount to be paid to the lender as a condition of full or partial prepayment of the loan.

Lock-in provisions are common in participating loans, where the lender's ability to convert its lien into an ownership interest, and conduit loans, where long-term investment is the premise, rather than simply a benefit, of the transaction. Such provisions appear to be generally enforceable and are, in any event, rarely negotiable. *See* discussion in § **8.06[D]**, this supplement.

Prepayment penalties are often justified as compensation to the lender for costs incurred as a result of loss of a long-term investment opportunity; however, enforceability of such provisions does not appear to depend on that rationale. Requirement for payment of a liquidated sum that bears no relationship to anticipated yield or for prepayment in an interest rate market more favorable to the lender than the stated interest under the existing loan does not appear to affect judicial enforceability. *See* Whitman, "Mortgage Prepayment: A Legal and Economic Analysis," 40 UCLA L. Rev. 851 (1993); Alexander, "Mortgage Prepayment: The Trial of Common Sense," 72 Cornell L. Rev. 288 (1987). Nonetheless, by far the more typical provision in recent loan transactions is a "yield maintenance" provision, which is intended, through a sometimes complex formula, to relate the required payment to the discounted value of the return the lender would have earned over the remaining term of the loan.

Given the importance of the issue to a long-term lender and the general fairness of this approach, such provisions will rarely be negotiable. What is more likely to trigger debate is whether a prepayment penalty should be collectible when repayment is not "voluntary," such as in cases of acceleration upon default, including violation of a due on sale provision, or as a result of casualty loss or condemnation of the real estate collateral.

Negotiation of exemption from a prepayment penalty in the event of loan acceleration upon a default is normally difficult, and arguably of little importance to the borrower. For loans that are (by contract or as a result of state anti-deficiency legislation) non-recourse, prepayment penalties are simply one more obligation of the borrower that cannot be collected. For recourse loans, the issue may be almost as academic.

Some courts have invalidated prepayment fees in the context of acceleration for violation of "due on sale" provisions, on the grounds that such prepayment is "involuntary." *See Tam v. California Fed. Sav. & Loan Ass'n*, 140 Cal. App. 3d 800, 189 Cal. Rptr. 775 (1983); *Slevin Container Corp. v. Provident Fed. Sav. & Loan Ass'n*, 98 Ill. App. 3d 646, 424 N.E.2d 939 (1981); Restatement of Property (Mortgages) § 6.3, Reporters' Note. Most lenders would disagree that transfer to a third party or to the lender by foreclosure is not within the control of the borrower, and again consider the issue to be non-negotiable.

It is with respect to acceleration or partial prepayment of the loan upon casualty loss or condemnation that the borrower's counsel is on strongest ground. If the loan documents are silent on the issue, common law generally nullifies application of prepayment fees in such circumstances. Assuming that the lender is not obligated by local law or provisions in the loan documents to apply insurance or condemnation proceeds to restoration of the real estate collateral (*see* § **8.03[C][7]**, *infra*, this supplement), courts have barred the imposition of prepayment fees on such amounts as are used to reduce or retire the debt. Restatement of Property (Mortgages) § 6.3. The reasoning of those decisions supports an argument by the borrower's attorney that, in the event that insurance or condemnation proceeds are insufficient to restore the premises, a prepayment penalty on down payment of the loan is not only truly involuntary, but also inequitable.

[C] Mortgage or Deed of Trust and Loan Agreement

[2] Dragnet and Spreader Clauses

Page 508, add new note 13.1 at end of second full paragraph:

[13.1] In most jurisdictions, dragnet clauses are enforceable and afford priority over subsequent lien holders only to the extent that future advances are either specifically described or, if generally referred to, are "similar in character" to the initial loan. *See* Restatement of Property (Mortgages) § 2.4, and articles and cases cited therein.

Page 509, add to note 14:

The law of fixtures or the "doctrine of accession" generally operates to include after-acquired improvements and fixtures as part of the original real estate collateral in a secured loan, even if the loan documents are silent on the issue. *See, e.g.*, 1 G. Nelson & D. Whitman, Real Estate Finance Law § 9.3 (3d ed. 1993). Accordingly, any intent to segregate such interests for separate financing or other purposes must be expressly stated in the loan documents.

[6] Extraordinary Risks

Page 527, add note 38.1 at end of carryover paragraph:

Industry reactions to the events of September 11, 2001, well illustrate both how quickly postures can change in the realm of extraordinary risks and how high are the stakes of the negotiations. At this writing, insurance against the consequences of acts of terrorism is either unavailable or economically utterly infeasible. Yet, a number of lenders have issued demands for the immediate addition of terrorism insurance, without reference to the market reality and under the auspices of their contract entitlement to dictate insurance requirements. Absent the kinds of constraints to customary provisions or commercially reasonableness discussed above (or some legislative intervention—through a combination of governmental coverage, requirements for private coverage or the denial of lender's rights to insist on such coverage), the posture of a borrower faced with such lender demands, however impractical, is, at best, uncertain.

[7] Insurance Proceeds and Condemnation Awards

Page 528, add to note 39:

In most jurisdictions, express provisions in loan documents providing for payment of insurance and condemnation proceeds to the lender are enforceable. *See* Restatement of Property (Mortgages) § 4.7. The Restatement, however, notes the "harshness" of such provisions, and suggests that, unless specifically provided to the contrary, such proceeds should be made available for restoration of the real estate collateral, subject to reasonable conditions protective of the lender's interest. Such an approach is typically negotiated and expressly provided in loan documents, as described below in this section. The Restatement also notes, in § 4.7, cmt. (e), that a mortgagor's waiver of the right to use funds for restoration may be unenforceable if the facts and circumstances indicate a violation of the mortgagee's duty of good faith and fair dealing. *See* § **8.02[C][3]**, *supra*, this supplement.

[15] Subordination Provisions

Page 549, add to note 47:

The Restatement of Property (Mortgages) § 7.7, summarizes the state of the law in most jurisdictions, noting generally that to be enforceable against an existing lender a subordination covenant must describe the subordinating loan with "reasonable specificity." Comment (b) to § 7.7 provides illustrations of the principle.

§ 8.03[D] COMMERCIAL REAL ESTATE TRANSACTIONS

[D] Assignment of Leases

[2] Assignment Language

Page 553, add to note 49:

There has been considerable scholarly commentary on the alternative legal characterizations of an assignment of rents, the effect of specific language in loan documents, the point in time when a lender can effect a remedy and the nature of that remedy, and analysis of cases that are frequently adjudicated by federal Bankruptcy Courts interpreting state law. See Restatement of Property (Mortgages) § 4.2. In most jurisdictions, whatever the technical analysis, an assignment of rents is collectable only upon default by the mortgagor under the loan documents, and judicially enforceable only by application for appointment of a receiver for the real property collateral.

§ 8.06 PARTICIPATION LOANS

[D] Relationship to Prepayment Rights

Page 591, add new note 57.1 at end of second to last sentence of first full paragraph:

[57.1] Prepayment penalties are generally enforceable in most jurisdictions. *See* discussion in § **8.03[B][4]**, this supplement. In comment (c) to the Restatement of Property (Mortgages) § 6.2, it is argued that, in view of the enforceability of "lock in" provisions and the ability of the mortgagor to avoid the sanction, the size of the prepayment penalty should be irrelevant. The same comment acknowledges that in certain circumstances (presumably only in the case of "involuntary" default) enforcement of such a penalty might violate principles of unconscionability or the duty of good faith and fair dealing.

§ 8.07 SECURITIZED LOANS

[D] Release/Defeasance

Page 595, add new note 59.1 at end of second sentence of the second full paragraph:

[59.1] The recent phenomenon of defeasance provisions in conduit loan transactional documents is reciprocal to a much more venerable, but little acknowledged, principle of common law that allows the mortgagee, as a matter of right, to substitute collateral, equal in value to the debt (and other loan fees and costs), that is the substantial equivalent to cash. *See* discussion, articles, and cases cited in Restatement of Property (Mortgages) § 6.2, cmt. (e). Express defeasance provisions, of course, spell out the lender's right to require replacement collateral and additional protections; it is unclear whether the borrower's common law right to release the lien on its property and substitute collateral (which need not be stated in the documents) would provide a more generous right to the mortgagee or whether a court would enforce this common law right in a commercial context, in which the loan documents express, in quite numbing detail, the parties' intent as to their respective rights and obligations. In any event, such a right need not be stated in the loan documents and would likely be resisted by the lender if it were suggested by the borrower.

Chapter 9
OPINION LETTERS IN REAL ESTATE LOAN TRANSACTIONS

Joel J. Goldberg
Robert T. Flick

§ 9.15 OPINION PRACTICE/CONDUCT

Page 641, add at end of section:

A sample legal opinion is included in this supplement as **Appendix 9C**. The sample opinion is neither a lender's form opinion nor a borrower's counsel's form opinion, but an example of a negotiated legal opinion that was delivered and accepted in an actual transaction. Consistent with the provisions of **§ 9.06** in the main volume, the opining law firm had lawyers admitted to practice in each of the jurisdictions whose law was expressly addressed in the opinion, and such lawyers participated in the negotiation and approval of the opinion.

This sample opinion, which addresses some topics not considered in the preceding provisions of this chapter (e.g., the perfection of security interests and guaranty and suretyship issues), is included merely as an example of a legal opinion and is not intended to serve as an "illustrative," "standard," "form," or "model" opinion. Further, although the sample opinion contains some opinion items, qualifications, and assumptions common to many opinions, it may not be appropriate in other transactions or typical of opinions delivered in all jurisdictions. The sample opinion, together with the balance of this chapter, should provide some guidance in negotiating legal opinions.

APPENDIX 9A
RELEVANT REPORTS

Page 644, add before "Pennsylvania":

North Carolina

Report of the Opinion Letter Subcommittee of the Commercial Law Committee of the Real Property Section of the North Carolina Bar Association (May 1993).

Report of the Legal Opinion Committee of the Business Law Section of the North Carolina Bar Association, "Third Party Legal Opinions in Business Transactions" (January 1, 1999).

Page 645, add at end of appendix:

Washington

Report on Third Party Legal Opinion Practice in the State of Washington by the Ad Hoc Committee on Third-Party Legal Opinions of the Business Law Section of the Washington State Bar Association (Fall 1998).

OPINIONS   APPENDIX 9C

Page 647, add new appendix:

APPENDIX 9C
SAMPLE LEGAL OPINION

[LAW FIRM LETTERHEAD]

[DATE]

_____
_____
_____

Re: $_____ Loan from _____ ("Lender") to _____ ("Borrower") concerning _____ (the "Project")

Ladies and Gentlemen:

A. **Introduction.**

We have acted as special counsel to Borrower, _____, a _____ ("Recourse Guarantor"), _____, a _____ ("General Partner"), _____, a _____ ("Managing Member"), and _____, a _____ ("Property Manager"), in connection with the $_____ loan ("Loan") to be made by Lender to Borrower pursuant to the terms and conditions of the Loan Documents (as defined below). This opinion is furnished to you pursuant to the request of Borrower. Capitalized terms which are used herein and are not otherwise defined herein shall have the meanings set forth in the Loan Documents.

B. **Documents and Items Reviewed.**

For purposes of rendering our opinions set forth herein, we have reviewed originals or copies of the following documents, each dated as of _____ ___, 200__:

1. Promissory Note (the "Note") made payable by the Borrower to the order of _____ (the "Lender") in the principal amount of $_____;

2. Deed of Trust, Security Agreement, Financing Statement, Fixture Filing, and Assignment of Leases, Rents, and Security Deposits made by Borrower to a trustee for the benefit of Lender (the "Deed of Trust");

3. Assignment of Leases, Rents, and Security Deposits from the Borrower to Lender (the "Assignment of Leases and Rents");

4. Account Security, Pledge, Assignment, and Control Agreement made by and among Borrower, Lender, and Property Manager (the "Account Agreement");

5. Lockbox Account Control Acknowledgment Agreement made by and between Borrower and _____ Bank, N.A. (the "Lockbox Agreement");

6. Manager's Consent and Subordination of Management Agreement made by Borrower and Property Manager to Lender (the "Manager's Subordination Agreement");

7. Environment Indemnity made by Recourse Guarantor to Lender (the "Environmental Indemnity");

8. Guaranty of Recourse Obligations made by Recourse Guarantor to Lender (the "Recourse Guaranty");

9. Uniform Commercial Code Financing Statements from the Borrower, as debtor, to Lender, as secured party (the "Financing Statements");

10. Rate Cap Pledge and Security Agreement from the Borrower to Lender ("RC Pledge Agreement"); and

11. Rate Cap Uniform Commercial Code Financing Statements from the Borrower, as debtor, to Lender, as secured party (the "RC Financing Statements").

The Deed of Trust, the Assignment of Leases and Rents, the Manager's Subordination Agreement, the Account Agreement, the Lockbox Agreement, the RC Pledge Agreement, the RC Financing Statements, and the Financing Statements are hereinafter collectively referred to as the "Security Documents." The Security Documents, together with the Note, the Environmental Indemnity, and the Recourse Guaranty, are hereinafter collectively referred to as the "Loan Documents."

In rendering our opinion we have also examined such certificates of public officials as we have deemed necessary for the purpose of our opinions herein expressed in Section D.1 below. With respect to our opinions set forth in Sections D.6(c) and (d) and D.14 below, we have relied solely upon, with your permission, our knowledge and that certain Borrower's Certificate attached hereto as Exhibit A and incorporated herein by reference ("Borrower's Certificate").

When we render a statement or opinion "to our knowledge" or concerning an item "known to us," or use words of similar import, such statement or opinion is based solely upon (a) the current, actual knowledge, without duty to investigate, of the attorneys within this firm who have given substantive legal attention to the representation of Borrower in connection with the Loan; (b) the contents of the Borrower's Certificate; and (c) such other investigation, if any, as may be specifically identified in this opinion letter.

C. **Assumptions.**

In rendering the opinions contained in this opinion letter, we have assumed, with your permission and without independent investigation or verification, that:

1. All natural persons involved in the Loan have sufficient legal capacity to enter into and perform their respective obligations under the Loan Documents or to carry out their roles with respect to the Loan.

2. Each party to the Loan other than Borrower, Property Manager, and Recourse Guarantor has satisfied all legal requirements that are applicable to it to the extent necessary to make the Loan Documents enforceable against it.

3. Each of the parties to the Loan other than Borrower, Property Manager, and Recourse Guarantor has complied with all legal requirements pertaining to its status as such status relates to its rights to enforce the Loan Documents.

4. Borrower holds the requisite title and rights to any property involved in the Loan that is designated as belonging to Borrower, including, without limitation, any property that is designated as collateral or security for the performance of the obligations of Borrower under the Loan Documents.

5. The conduct of each of the parties to the Loan complies with any and all applicable requirements of good faith, fair dealing, and conscionability.

6. There has not been any mutual mistake of fact, fraud, duress, or undue influence.

7. All statutes, judicial and administrative decisions, and rules and regulations of governmental agencies, applicable to this opinion, are generally available to lawyers practicing in the States of California and New York and are in a format that makes legal research reasonably feasible.

8. Each party to the Loan Documents other than Borrower, Recourse Guarantor, and Property Manager has full power and authority to execute, deliver, and perform such Loan Documents, and each party to the Loan Documents other than Borrower, Recourse Guarantor, and Property Manager has duly authorized the execution, delivery, and performance of such Loan Documents by all necessary action.

9. All documents submitted to us as originals are authentic, and all documents submitted to us as certified, conformed, or photostatic copies conform to authentic original documents.

10. The descriptions of the real property and the personal property contained in the Loan Documents are legally sufficient and adequate under applicable law (including, without limitation, the Uniform Commercial Code, as presently in effect in the State of California or the State of New York ("UCC")) to enable a subsequent purchaser or mortgagee to identify such property.

11. The terms and conditions of the Loan as reflected in the Loan Documents have not been amended, modified, or supplemented by any other written agreement or written understanding of the parties or written waiver of any of the material provisions of the Loan Documents. To our knowledge, without independent investigation, nothing has come to our attention that leads us to believe that we are not justified in making the foregoing assumption.

APPENDIX 9C COMMERCIAL REAL ESTATE TRANSACTIONS

12. Except for such consents, approvals, authorizations, registrations, declarations, and filings as have heretofore been obtained or made, no consents or approvals of, authorizations by, or registrations, declarations, or filings with any governmental authority are required for any party, other than Borrower, Recourse Guarantor, or Property Manager, to execute, deliver, or perform its obligations under the Loan Documents to which it is a party.

13. The Deed of Trust and the Financing Statements will be recorded and filed, as applicable, with the County Recorder of the county in which the Property is located and with the California Secretary of State, and all recordation or filing charges specified herein will be paid thereon.

14. Lender has given "value" (as defined in the California Commercial Code ("CCC") and in the New York Commercial Code) to the Borrower for the Note and for the security interests granted under the Loan Documents.

15. All tangible personal property of Borrower in which a security interest is granted under the Loan Documents (other than accounts or goods of a type normally used in more than one jurisdiction) is located at the Property.

D. **Opinions.**

Based on the foregoing and upon such investigation as we have deemed necessary, and subject to the qualifications and exceptions herein contained, we are of the opinion that:

1. (a) The Borrower is a limited partnership duly organized, validly existing, and in good standing under the laws of the State of Delaware and is authorized to do business and in good standing in the State of California. Borrower has the requisite power to own its properties and to carry on its business as now being conducted.
   (b) Recourse Guarantor is a corporation, duly organized, validly existing, and in good standing under the laws of the State of Maryland and is authorized to do business and in good standing in the State of California.
   (c) The Property Manager is a corporation, duly organized, validly existing, and in good standing under the laws of the State of Maryland and is authorized to do business and is in good standing in the State of California.
   (d) The General Partner is a limited liability company, duly organized, validly existing, and in good standing under the laws of the State of Delaware and is authorized to do business and is in good standing in the State of California.
   (e) The Managing Member is a limited partnership, duly authorized, validly existing, and in good standing under the laws of the State of Delaware.

2. Under the Delaware Revised Uniform Limited Partnership Act, 6 Del. C. Sec. 17-101 *et seq.*, (the "ALP Act") and the limited partnership agreement of Borrower ("Borrower's LP Agreement"), Borrower has all nec-

essary limited partnership power and authority to execute and deliver the Loan Documents to which Borrower is party, and to perform all of Borrower's obligations thereunder. Under the LP Act and the Borrower's LP Agreement, the execution and delivery by Borrower of the Loan Documents to which Borrower is a party, and the performance by Borrower of its obligations thereunder, have been duly authorized by all necessary limited partnership action on the part of Borrower.

3. The transfer of the Project to Borrower by Managing Member has been duly authorized by all necessary limited liability company, partnership, and corporate action, as applicable, and no consent from any of the constituent limited partners of Managing Member is required with respect to the transfer of the Project from Managing Member to Borrower or the execution and delivery of the Loan Documents by Borrower or Recourse Guarantor or the performance by Borrower or Recourse Guarantor of their respective obligations under the Loan Documents.

4. The execution and delivery of the Environmental Indemnity and the Recourse Guaranty by the Recourse Guarantor have been duly authorized by all necessary limited liability company, partnership, and corporate action, as applicable.

5. The execution and delivery of the Manager's Subordination Agreement by Property Manager have been duly authorized by all necessary limited liability company, partnership, and corporate action, as applicable.

6. The execution, delivery, and performance by the Borrower and Recourse Guarantor of the Loan Documents to which it is a party does not (a) conflict with or result in a breach of any of the terms, conditions, or provisions of, or constitute a default under, the partnership agreement, partnership certificate, articles of incorporation, by-laws, trust agreement, or trust certificate, as applicable, of the Borrower or Recourse Guarantor; (b) contravene any law, statute, or regulation of the United States of America or the States of New York or California; (c) violate any order, writ, injunction, or decree of which we have knowledge, issued by any court or governmental authority of the United States of America or the States of New York or California or any agency or political subdivision of any of them to which the Borrower or Recourse Guarantor is subject; or (d) to our knowledge, conflict with or result in any breach of any of the terms or provisions of, or constitute a default under, or result in the creation or imposition of (or the obligation to create or impose) any lien other than the lien of the Deed of Trust and the Assignment of Leases and Rents upon any of the assets or properties of the Borrower or Recourse Guarantor pursuant to the terms of any material indenture, mortgage, deed of trust, agreement, contract, or instrument known to us to which the Borrower or Recourse Guarantor is a party or by which it or any of its assets or properties is bound.

7. The Loan Documents to which Borrower is a party are the valid and binding obligations of Borrower, enforceable against Borrower in accordance with their respective terms.

8. The Environmental Indemnity and the Recourse Guaranty are the legal, valid, and binding obligations of the Recourse Guarantor, enforceable against the Recourse Guarantor in accordance with their terms.

9. The Manager's Subordination Agreement is the legal, valid, and binding obligation of the Property Manager, enforceable against the Property Manager in accordance with its terms.

10. The Deed of Trust is in form sufficient to create a lien on the real property collateral described therein ("Deed of Trust Collateral") in favor of the trustee thereunder for the benefit of the beneficiary thereunder, and the Financing Statements and the RC Financing Statements are in form sufficient to create and perfect a security interest in favor of Lender as secured party, with respect to those items of collateral described in the Financing Statements or the RC Financing Statements in which a security interest may be perfected by filing ("UCC Collateral"), in each case to secure the full amount of the secured obligations described in the Deed of Trust. In order to provide constructive notice of the lien created by the Deed of Trust and in order to perfect the security interest created by the Financing Statements or the RC Financing Statements with respect to the UCC Collateral, it is necessary to record the Deed of Trust in the Official Records of _____ County, State of California, and to file the Financing Statements in the office of the California Secretary of State pursuant to the recording and filing systems established pursuant to applicable California law. Regarding fixtures included in the UCC Collateral, we have assumed that such fixtures are located on the Deed of Trust Collateral and that the Borrower had or will have an interest of record in the Deed of Trust Collateral at the time of filing and recording of such Fixture Filing. Except for the filing of periodic continuation statements as required by the UCC and except for the recording of a Notice of Intent to Preserve Security Interest pursuant to California Civil Code Sections 880.310 880.370, it is not necessary to re-record, re-register, or re-file the Deed of Trust or the Financing Statement or to record, register, or file any other or additional documents, instruments, or statements in order to maintain the priority of the liens and security interests created thereby; provided, however, that additional financing statements and fixture filings may be required to be filed if Borrower changes its name, identity, or corporate structure, or the jurisdiction in which its place of business (or, if it has more than one place of business, its chief executive office) or the UCC Collateral is located. There are no mortgage taxes or filing fees payable upon the recording and filing of such document except: (i) nominal recording and filing fees payable to the County Recorder of _____ County, California, and to the California Secretary of State in connection therewith; (ii) any transfer taxes assessed in connection with any transfer of the Deed of Trust Collateral or interest therein (other than the transfer that occurs upon the execution and delivery of the Deed of Trust); and (iii) any fee or charge payable to any entity whose services may have been used to assist in such recordation and filing. We express no opinion, however, with respect to any income, franchise, sales, withholding, real or personal property, business license, or other tax that

may result from the transactions contemplated by the Loan Documents or the performance of the obligations described therein, including the payment of the indebtedness secured by the Deed of Trust.

11. The Assignment of Leases and Rents is in proper form so as to comply with the recording requirements of the State of California.

12. After the due execution and delivery of the Deed of Trust by Borrower and the unconditional funding of the Loan by Lender, the Deed of Trust will create a lien upon the real property portion of the Deed of Trust Collateral. After the due execution and delivery of the Security Instrument and the Financing Statements, and upon the proper filing of the Financing Statements in the Office of the Secretary of State of the State of California, the security interest created by the Security Instrument and the Financing Statements in the UCC Collateral will be perfected to the extent a security interest in the UCC Collateral can be perfected by the filing of a UCC-1 financing statement in the State of California under the provisions of the UCC.

13. After the due execution and delivery of the RC Pledge and the RC Financing Statements, and upon the proper filing of the RC Financing Statements in the Office of the Secretary of State of the State of New York, the security interest created by the RC Pledge and the RC Financing Statements in the collateral described therein will be perfected to the extent a security interest in such collateral can be perfected by the filing of a UCC-1 financing statement in the State of New York under the provisions of the UCC.

14. The Account Agreement is effective to create in favor of Lender a valid security interest under the Uniform Commercial Code in effect in the State of New York on the date hereof (the "NY UCC") (including the NY UCC as made applicable to any security entitlements with respect to book-entry securities (as such term is defined in 31 CFR § 357.2) pursuant to 31 CFR § 357.11) in all of Borrower's right, title, and interest in the security entitlements in the accounts listed on <u>Exhibit B</u> attached hereto (the "Security Accounts"). "Security entitlement" has the meaning set forth in § 8-102(a)(17) of the UCC with respect to "financial assets" (as defined in § 8-102(a)(9) of the UCC) and the meaning set forth in 31 CFR § 357.2 with respect to "book-entry securities" (as defined in 31 CFR § 357.2).

15. Based solely upon our review of our firm's internal litigation docket and the Borrower's Certificate, we have no knowledge of any pending or threatened litigation or proceedings against Borrower, Recourse Guarantor, Property Manager, Managing Member, or General Partner concerning the Project.

16. The State of California has no law pursuant to which a lien against any assets or properties of Borrower (whether real, personal, mixed, tangible, or intangible) superior to the lien created by the Deed of Trust could arise as a result of a violation of environmental laws or regulations of such State. No environmental law or regulation of the State of California would require any remedial or removal action or certification of nonapplicability as a condition to the granting of the Deed of Trust, the foreclosure or other

APPENDIX 9C   **COMMERCIAL REAL ESTATE TRANSACTIONS**

enforcement of the Security Documents, or the sale of any assets or properties of Borrower (whether real, personal, mixed, tangible, or intangible) located in the State of California; provided, however, that:

    a. We assume for purposes of the opinion contained in this sentence that the Project is not a "border zone property" or "hazardous waste property" as defined and used in California Health & Safety Code Sections 25220 through 25241 and is not and will not be otherwise subject to classification or restriction under those sections (to our knowledge, based solely upon our review of the Borrower's Certificate, the Project has not previously been designated as a "border zone property" or a "hazardous waste property");

    b. We note that certain disclosures regarding the presence or release of hazardous substances are required under California law in connection with a proposed conveyance or lease of real property, including, without limitation, under California Health & Safety Code Section 25359.7, and that such disclosures could cause a prospective purchaser or lender, as a practical matter, to condition its purchase of, or loan secured by, the Project upon the prior completion of remediation or removal activities or a certification of nonapplicability with respect to the Project (to our knowledge, based solely upon our review of the Borrower's Certificate, no such disclosure has been given by Borrower to Lender); and

    c. We note that certain notifications regarding the release of hazardous substances are required under California law, including, without limitation, under the California Environmental Responsibility Act (California Civil Code Section 850 et seq.), and that such notifications could cause a prospective purchaser or lender, as a practical matter, to condition its purchase of, or loan secured by, the Project upon the prior completion of remediation or removal activities or a certification of nonapplicability with respect to the Project (to our knowledge, based solely upon our review of the Borrower's Certificate, no such notification has been given by Borrower to Lender).

17. Except as expressly referenced in this opinion letter, no approval, authorization, or other action by, or filing with, any governmental authority of the United States of America or the States of California or New York is required for the valid execution or delivery by the Borrower of any of the Loan Documents or the performance by Borrower of its payment obligations thereunder.

18. The Loan, as made, will not violate any applicable usury laws of the State of California, assuming for the purposes of this opinion that the internal laws of the State of California were applied.

OPINIONS APPENDIX 9C

19. The Loan, as made, will not violate any applicable usury laws of the State of New York, assuming for the purposes of this opinion that the internal laws of the State of New York were applied.

E. **Bankruptcy and Insolvency Exception.**

Our opinions are subject to the effect of bankruptcy, insolvency, reorganization, receivership, moratorium, and other similar laws affecting the rights and remedies of creditors generally. This exception includes, without limitation:

1. The Federal Bankruptcy Code and thus comprehends, among others, matters of turn-over, automatic stay, avoiding powers, fraudulent transfer, preference, discharge, conversion of a non-recourse obligation into a recourse claim, limitations on ipso facto and anti-assignment clauses, and the coverage of pre-petition security agreements applicable to property acquired after a petition is filed;

2. All other Federal and state bankruptcy, insolvency, reorganization, receivership, moratorium, arrangement, and assignment for the benefit of creditors laws that affect the rights and remedies of creditors generally (not just creditors of specific types of debtors);

3. State fraudulent transfer and fraudulent conveyance laws; and

4. Judicially developed doctrines relevant to any of the foregoing laws (but excluding the substantive consolidation of entities, which is covered in a separate opinion).

F. **Equitable Principles Limitation.**

Our opinions are subject to the effect of general principles of equity, whether applied by a court of law or equity. This limitation includes, without limitation, the following principles:

1. Governing the availability of specific performance, injunctive relief, or other equitable remedies, which generally place the award of such remedies, subject to certain guidelines, in the discretion of the court to which application for such relief is made;

2. Affording equitable defenses (e.g., waiver, laches, and estoppel) against a party seeking enforcement;

3. Requiring good faith and fair dealing in the performance and enforcement of a contract by the party seeking its enforcement;

4. Requiring commercial reasonableness in the performance and enforcement of an agreement by the party seeking enforcement of the contract; and

5. Affording defenses based upon the unconscionability of the enforcing party's conduct after the parties have entered into the contract.

G. <u>Generic Exception and Assurance.</u>

Certain remedies, waivers, and other provisions of the Loan Documents may not be enforceable; nevertheless, subject to the limitations expressed elsewhere in this opinion, upon a material default by Borrower in the payment of principal or interest thereon as provided in the Note or upon a material default by the Borrower in the performance of any other material covenant of the Loan Documents, such unenforceability will not preclude (1) the acceleration of the obligation of the Borrower to repay such principal and interest, (2) enforcement in accordance with applicable law of the assignment of rents set forth in the Loan Documents, (3) the foreclosure in accordance with applicable law of the security interests in the described collateral created by the Loan Documents, and (4) judicial enforcement in accordance with applicable law of the obligation of Borrower to repay such principal or interest as provided in the Note.

H. <u>Additional Qualifications.</u>

To the extent the law of the State of California or the State of New York applies any of the following rules to one or more of the provisions of a Loan Document, our opinion is subject to the effect of generally applicable rules of law that:

1. Limit or affect the enforcement of provisions of a contract that purport to require waiver of the obligations of good faith, fair dealing, and commercial reasonableness;

2. Provide the forum selection clauses in contracts are not necessarily binding on the court(s) in the forum selected;

3. Limit the availability of a remedy under certain circumstances where another remedy has been elected;

4. Limit the right of a creditor to use force or cause a breach of the peace in enforcing rights;

5. Relate to the sale or disposition of collateral or the requirements of a commercially reasonable sale;

6. Limit the enforceability of provisions releasing, exculpating, or exempting a party from, or requiring indemnification of a party for, liability for its own action or inaction, to the extent the action or inaction involves gross negligence, recklessness, willful misconduct, or unlawful conduct;

7. May, where less than all of a contract may be unenforceable, limit the enforceability of the balance of the contract to circumstances in which the unenforceable portion is not an essential part of the agreed exchange;

8. Govern and afford judicial discretion regarding the determination of damages and entitlement to attorneys' fees and other costs;

9. May, in the absence of a waiver or consent, discharge a guarantor to the extent that (a) action by a creditor impairs the value of collateral securing guaranteed debt to the detriment of the guarantor, or (b) guaranteed debt is materially modified;

10. May permit a party who has materially failed to render or offer performance required by the contract to cure that failure unless (a) permitting a cure would unreasonably hinder the aggrieved party from making substitute arrangements for performance, or (b) it was important in the circumstances to the aggrieved party that performance occur by the date stated in the contract;

11. Limit or affect the enforceability of a waiver of a right of redemption;

12. Impose limitations on attorneys' or trustee's fees;

13. Limit or affect the enforceability of any provision that purports to prevent any party from becoming a mortgagee in possession notwithstanding enforcement actions taken under the Loan Documents; and

14. Limit or affect the enforceability of provisions for late charges, prepayment charges, or yield maintenance charges, and acceleration of future amounts due (other than principal) without appropriate discount to present value, liquidated damages, late charges, prepayment charges and increased interest rates upon default, and other "penalties"; provided, however, that the qualification contained in this Section H.14 shall not limit our opinions set forth in Section D.18 or Section D.19 above.

I. **Additional Qualifications—California.**

We express no opinion as to the validity or enforceability of any provisions of the Loan Documents that:

1. Require a borrower to provide hazard insurance coverage against risks in an amount exceeding the replacement value of any improvements to real property;

2. Impose requirements respecting impound accounts in conflict with applicable law;

3. Provide for the application of insurance or condemnation proceeds to reduce indebtedness;

4. Purport to make any assignment of rents, issues, and profits from the Deed of Trust Collateral enforceable without the lender taking steps to enforce in accordance with applicable law or which purport to allow the lender to collect rents, issues, and profits and not apply those collections to the indebtedness secured by the Loan Documents;

5. Contain a waiver of any party's statutory right to reinstate a secured obligation by paying the delinquent amounts of the fully accelerated debt at any time prior to the time provided by statute or that contain a waiver of any right of redemption;

6. Are in conflict with any laws governing foreclosure and disposition procedures regarding any collateral or in conflict with any limitations on attorneys' or trustees' fees;

7. Indemnifies any party against its own negligence or willful misconduct;

8. Are in conflict with the real property antideficiency, fair value, security first, and one form of action provisions of California law;

9. Provide for the acceleration of any indebtedness upon any transfer or further encumbrance of any of the collateral for any loan, or upon a change of ownership of any entity which directly or indirectly owns any interest in any such collateral, except to the extent that (a) such provisions are made enforceable pursuant to the federal preemption afforded by the Garn–St. Germain Depository Institutions Act of 1982, as set forth at 12 U.S.C. 1701j-3 and the regulations adopted pursuant thereto or (b) enforcement is reasonably necessary to protect against impairment of the lender's security or an increase in the risk of default;

10. [intentionally omitted];
11. Provide that time is of the essence;
12. Provide for the confession of judgment;
13. Contain a waiver of (i) broadly or vaguely stated rights; (ii) the benefits of statutory, regulatory, or constitutional rights, unless and to the extent the statute, regulation, or constitution explicitly allows waiver; (iii) unknown future defenses; and (iv) rights to damages;
14. Attempt to change or waive rules of evidence or fix the method or quantum of proof to be applied in litigation or similar proceedings;
15. Select the forum for the resolution of any disputes or consent to the jurisdiction of any jurisdiction (both as to personal jurisdiction and subject matter jurisdiction); or
16. Appoint one party as an attorney-in-fact for an adverse party.

With respect to the opinions and qualifications set forth herein, you should be aware of the following provisions of California law:

a. Section 726 of the California Code of Civil Procedure provides that any action to recover on a debt or other right secured by a mortgage or a deed of trust on real property must comply with the requirements of that section, which requirements relate to and specify the procedures for the sale of encumbered property, the application of proceeds, the rendition in certain cases of a deficiency judgment, and other related matters. We advise you that in such an action or proceeding, the debtor may require the creditor to exhaust all of its security before a personal judgment may be obtained against the debtor for a deficiency. We also advise you that failure to comply with the provisions of Section 726 (including an attempt to exercise a right to set off with respect to any funds of Borrower that may be deposited with you from time to time and with respect to which you do not hold a perfected security interest) may result in loss of your lien on the real property collateral. *See, e.g., Walker Community Bank,* 10 Cal. 3d 729, 111 Cal. Rptr. 897, 518 P.2d 329 (1974); *Security Pacific National Bank v. Wozab,* 51 Cal. 3d 991, 275 Cal. Rptr. 201, 800 P.2d 557 (1990). For example, in *Security Pacific National Bank v. Wozab, supra,* the lender was held to have lost its lien on real property security by exercising a right of setoff with respect to funds of the borrower deposited with the lender and as to which the lender did not have a security interest.

b. Section 580b of the California Code of Civil Procedure provides that no deficiency judgment shall be rendered upon a purchase-money obligation in favor of the vendor arising from the sale of real property where such purchase-money obligation is secured by a lien on the real property purchased from the vendor, or in favor of a lender where the proceeds of the loan are used to purchase a one- to four-family dwelling occupied entirely or in part by the borrower and where such loan is secured by a lien on such dwelling.

c. Section 580d of the California Code of Civil Procedure provides that no deficiency judgment shall be rendered upon a note secured by a deed of trust or mortgage on real property after sale of the real property under the power of sale contained in such deed of trust or mortgage.

d. Section 2924c of the California Civil Code provides that whenever the maturity of an obligation secured by a deed of trust or mortgage on real property is accelerated by reason of a default in the payment of interest or in the payment of any installment of principal or other sums secured thereby, or by reason of failure of the trustor or mortgagor to pay taxes, assessments, or insurance premiums, the trustor or mortgagor and certain other specified persons have the right, to be exercised at any time within the reinstatement period described in such section, to cure such default by paying the entire amount then due (including certain reasonable costs and expenses incurred in enforcing such obligations but excluding any principal amount that would not then be due had no default occurred) and thereby cure the default and reinstate such deed of trust or mortgage and the obligations secured thereby to the same effect as if no acceleration has occurred. If the power of sale in the deed of trust or mortgage is not to be exercised, such reinstatement right may be exercised at any time prior to entry of the decree of foreclosure.

e. Section 2938 of the California Civil Code deals with the creation, perfection, and enforcement of an assignment of any interest in leases, rents, issues, or profits made in connection with an obligation secured by real property and provides specific provisions regarding the enforcement of such an assignment. We note that the statute has not yet been interpreted judicially. We also note that the only method that is clearly established under California law for enforcement of an assignment of rents is by appointment of a receiver by a court in an action for specific performance of the provisions of the Financing Documents that provide for an assignment of rents.

f. Section 725.5 of the California Code of Civil Procedure authorizes, under certain limited circumstances, a real estate–secured commercial lender to waive its lien against a parcel of "environmentally impaired" security (as therein defined) and sue the borrower without foreclosing on the real property collateral for the loan.

g. Section 736 of the California Code of Civil Procedure permits a lender, under certain limited circumstances, to sue for breach of contract relating to any "environmental provisions" (as therein defined) concerning real property security without foreclosing on the real property security or in an action brought following foreclosure, whether judicial or non-judicial.

h. Sections 580a and 726 of the California Code of Civil Procedure impose fair value limitations on the amount of the deficiency judgment that can be recovered following the foreclosure.

i. Sections 2889 and 2903 through 2905 of the California Civil Code and Sections 729.010 through 729.090 of the California Code of Civil Procedure grant certain redemption rights to persons having an interest in property subject to a lien and prevent the parties to the contract from restraining the right of redemption from a lien.

j. The provisions of Sections 564 *et seq.* of the California Code of Civil Procedure prescribe the manner and circumstances under which appointments of receivers are authorized.

k. California Code of Civil Procedure Section 631(d) provides that a court may, in its discretion upon just terms, allow a trial by jury although there may have been a waiver of trial by jury.

l. Section 2954.5 of the California Civil Code imposes, among other things, certain notice requirements as a condition precedent to the right of a real property secured lender to assess a default, delinquency, or late payment charge on a delinquent loan payment.

m. Section 2954.1 of the California Civil Code provides, among other things, that a lender who maintains an impound account for the payment of taxes and assessments on real property, insurance premiums, or other purposes related to such property shall not (i) require the borrower to deposit in such an account in any month an amount in excess of that which would be permitted under the statute, or (ii) require the sums maintained in such account to exceed at any time the amount or amounts reasonably necessary to pay such obligations as they become due.

n. Section 2955(a) of the California Civil Code provides, among other things, that, subject to the exceptions set forth in California Civil Code Section 2955(b), money held by a beneficiary of a deed of trust on California real property in an impound account for the payment of taxes or assessments or insurance premiums or other purposes on or relating to the property shall be retained in California and, if invested, shall be invested only with residents of California or with entities engaged in business within California. We assume for purposes of this opinion, with Lender's permission, that (one) Lender is a bank, bank subsidiary, bank holding company, or subsidiary of a bank holding company doing business under the authority of and in accordance with the laws of the United States or the State of New York relating to banks, as evidenced by a license, certificate, or charter issued by the United States or the State of New York, (two) the Deed of Trust will constitute, upon due recordation, a first lien on the Property, and (three) any such impound account will be held in a depository institution insured by the Federal Deposit Insurance Corporation, and that accordingly Lender is exempt from the restrictions of Section 2955(a).

o. The right of Lender under the Loan Documents to apply proceeds collected under fire or other property insurance policies or to apply awards or damages in condemnation proceedings against the secured indebtedness may be subject to a limitation (including, without limitation, under Section 1265.225 of the California Code of Civil Procedure) upon such application where and to the extent that the security under the Loan Documents is not impaired. This limitation does not affect or limit the right of Lender to apply such proceeds to the repair of the encumbered property in accordance with the provisions of the Loan Documents or to receive and control disbursement of such proceeds.

p. Section 1670.5 of the California Civil Code allows a court to refuse to enforce all or part of any contract or clause in a contract which, as a matter of law, is found to have been unconscionable at the time made or contrary to public policy.

q. Section 882.020 of the California Civil Code provides that unless the lien of a mortgage, deed of trust, or other instrument that creates a security interest of record in real property to secure a debt or other obligation has earlier expired on the date provided by California Civil Code Section 2911 (*i.e.*, the last day upon which an action can be brought upon the principal obligation), the lien expires at, and is not enforceable by action for foreclosure commenced, power of sale exercised, or any other means asserted after, the later of the following times: (i) if the final maturity date or the last date fixed for payment of the debt or performance of the obligation is ascertainable from the record, 10 years after that date; (ii) if the final maturity date or the last date fixed for payment of the debt or performance of the obligation is not ascertainable from the record, or if there is no final maturity date or last date fixed for payment of the debt or performance of the obligation, 60 years after the date the instrument that created the security interest was recorded; and (iii) if a notice of intent to preserve the security interest is recorded within the time prescribed in clause (i) or (ii) above, 10 years after the date the notice is recorded.

r. To the extent that the Loan Documents provide for the payment of attorneys' fees in litigation, Section 1717 of the California Civil Code regarding the requirement that such attorneys' fees be reasonable and providing that such provisions extend to both parties to the litigation, whether or not by their express terms they benefit only one party.

J. **Additional Qualifications—Perfection of Security Interests Under the UCC.**

With respect to the perfection of security interests in the UCC Collateral under the UCC and the perfection of security interests in the collateral described in the RC Financing Statements ("RC Collateral"), you should also be aware of, and our opinions are subject to and limited by, the following provisions:

1. We express no opinion as to the perfection of any security interest in any portion of the UCC Collateral or the RC Collateral that is not governed by, or that is excluded from, or which is not perfected by the filing of a financing statement under the Division 9 of the UCC.

2. We have assumed that the debtor has "rights" in the UCC Collateral and the RC Collateral and that "value" has been given, as contemplated by Section 9203 of the UCC.

3. We have assumed that none of the UCC Collateral or the RC Collateral consists of consumer goods or is subject to a statute or treaty of the United States which provides for or which specifies a place of filing different from that specified in the UCC for the filing of the security interest, or any other items excluded from the coverage of the UCC by Section 9104 thereof.

4. We call to your attention the fact that the perfection of a security interest in "Proceeds" (as defined in the UCC) of collateral is governed and restricted by Section 9306 of the UCC.

5. We have assumed that the security interests in any portion of the collateral constituting the "inventory of a retail merchant" (within the meaning of Section 9102 of the UCC) secures a debt as to which the secured party has made no restriction as to use of funds, other than those

which are commercially reasonable and made in good faith, as contemplated by Section 9102(5)(b) of the UCC.

6. We note that the law is not well developed with respect to the specificity of description necessary to create a valid security interest in personal property. We express no opinion as to whether the phrase "all property" or similarly general phrases would be held to describe any particular item or items of collateral.

7. In the case of any portion of the UCC Collateral or RC Collateral which becomes subject to a security interest after the date hereof, Section 552 of the Federal Bankruptcy Code limits the extent to which property acquired by a debtor after the commencement of a case under the Federal Bankruptcy Code may be subject to a security interest arising from a security agreement entered into by the debtor before the commencement of such a case.

8. The perfection of any such security interest will be terminated as to any portion of the UCC Collateral or RC Collateral acquired by the Borrower more than four months after the Borrower so changes its name, identity, or corporate structure so as to make the Financing Statements misleading, unless new, appropriate financing statements indicating the new name, identity, or corporate structure of the Borrower are properly filed before the expiration of such four months.

9. We express no opinion as to the validity, binding effect, or enforceability of any provision in the Loan Documents that purports (i) to permit any person or entity to sell or otherwise dispose of, or purchase, any property or collateral subject thereto, or enforce any other right or remedy thereunder (including, without limitation, any self-help or taking possession remedy), except in compliance with the UCC and other applicable laws; (ii) to limit the ability of any debtor or any other person or entity to transfer voluntarily or involuntarily (by way of sale, creation of a security interest, attachment, levy, garnishment, or other judicial process) its right, title, or interest in or to any collateral subject thereto, as contemplated by Section 9-311 of the UCC; or (iii) to establish standards for the performance of the obligations of good faith, diligence, reasonableness, and care prescribed by the UCC.

10. We express no opinion with respect to the enforceability of the security interests under the Loan Documents to the extent the security interests are in collateral that is acquired after the date of this letter and involve circumstances in which such security interests are deemed to be taken as security for an antecedent debt and other than for new value under Section 9108 of the UCC.

11. The effect of the provisions of the UCC that require a secured party, in any disposition of personal property collateral, to act in good faith and in a commercially reasonable manner.

12. We call to your attention that under the UCC, events occurring subsequent to the date hereof may affect any security interests subject to the UCC and one or more of the following severally applicable provisions

may affect the security interest of the Lender including, but not limited to, factors of the type identified in Section 9-306 with respect to proceeds; Section 9-103 with respect to changes in the location of the collateral and the location of the debtor; Section 9-316 with respect to subordination agreements; Section 9-403 with respect to continuation statements; and Sections 9-307, 9-308, and 9-309 with respect to subsequent purchasers of the collateral. In addition, actions taken by a secured party (e.g., releasing or assigning the security interest, delivering possession of the collateral to the debtor or another person, and voluntarily subordinating a security interest) may affect the validity, perfection, or priority of a security interest.

13. In the case of any instrument, chattel paper, account, or general intangible which is itself secured by other property, we express no opinion with respect to the Lender's rights in and to such underlying property.

14. We call to your attention that the American Law Institute and the National Conference of Commissioners on Uniform State Law have approved a revised version of Article 9, with conforming amendments to Articles 1, 2, 2a, 4, 5, 6, 7, and 8, of the Uniform Commercial Code ("Revised Article 9"), which substantially changes the law governing the creation and perfection of security interests. Revised Article 9 has been adopted in California and New York legislatures and will become effective on July 1, 2001. The opinions set forth herein are based solely on the law in effect on the date hereof; accordingly, we express no opinion as to the effect of Revised Article 9 on the validity, perfection, or priority of the security interest.

K. **Additional Qualifications—Guaranty and Suretyship.**

1. We advise you that, under certain circumstances, a guaranty executed by (i) a general partner (including a general partner through one or more intermediate partnerships) of a partnership borrower or (ii) a shareholder of a corporate principal obligor may not be enforceable as an obligation separate and distinct from the guaranteed obligations described therein if it is determined that the borrower is merely an alter ego or nominee of the guarantor and that the "true" borrower is the guarantor. See, e.g., Riddle v. Lushing, 203 Cal. App. 2d 831 (1962); Valinda Builders v. Vissner, 230 Cal. App. 2d 106 (1964). This is the case even if the loan is non-recourse to the borrower. Westinghouse Credit Corp. v. Barton, 789 F. Supp. 1043 (C.D. Cal. 1992). If a guarantor is deemed to be liable as a principal, and, notwithstanding our opinion regarding the parties' choice of New York law, California law is held to apply to the interpretation and enforcement of the Recourse Guaranty, it is likely that the guarantor will also be entitled to the rights and defenses otherwise available to a principal, including the protection of California's one action and antideficiency laws. For purposes of this opinion, we have assumed, without independent investigation, that neither Borrower nor Recourse Guarantor would be deemed to be the alter ego or nominee of any of the others.

2. We advise you of California statutory provisions and case law to the effect that, in certain circumstances, a guarantor may be exonerated

if the creditor materially alters the original obligation of the principal without the consent of the guarantor, elects remedies for default that impair the subrogation rights of the guarantor against the principal, or otherwise takes any action without notifying the guarantor that materially prejudices the guarantor. However, there is authority to the effect that a guarantor may validly waive such rights if the waivers are expressly set forth in the guaranty. *See, e.g., Krueger v. Bank of America,* 145 Cal. App. 3d 204 (1983); Section 2856 of the California Civil Code ("CCC"). Section 2856(b) of the CCC states that any language that expressly sets forth a waiver of the suretyship rights or defenses set forth in Section 2856(a) of the CCC shall be effective, and sets forth specific language which is deemed to create an effective waiver of the guarantor's defense to a recovery by the creditor by reason of the creditor's election of remedies. We note to you, however, a decision of the California Court of Appeal, *Cathay Bank v. Lee,* 14 Cal. App. 4th 1533, 18 Cal. Rptr. 2d 420 (1993), which invalidated certain waivers contained in a guaranty because the Court of Appeal found that the language of the waivers was not sufficiently explicit in informing the guarantor of the nature of the defense purportedly being waived. The reasoning of the *Cathay Bank* opinion could be applied to, and thus could affect, all waivers contained in any Loan Document. We express no opinion with respect to the effect of (a) any modification to or amendment of the guarantied obligations that materially increases such obligations; (b) any election of remedies by Lender following the occurrence of an event of default; or (c) any other action by Lender that materially prejudices a guarantor, if, in any such instance, such modification, election, or action occurs without the consent of or notice to such guarantor and without granting to such guarantor an opportunity to cure any such default.

L. **Limitations.**

1. We express no opinion with respect to the applicability of the laws of any jurisdiction other than the State of California, the State of New York, the corporate law of the State of Maryland, the Revised Uniform Limited Partnership Act of the State of Delaware, the Limited Liability Company Act of the State of Delaware, and all federal laws, to the extent applicable. Further, this opinion is predicated solely upon laws and regulations in existence as of the present date and as they presently apply and we assume no obligation to advise you of changes that may hereafter be brought to our attention. Without limitation, we express no opinion regarding the laws of the State of Texas.

2. We express no opinion with regard to any laws, statutes, ordinances, rules, or regulations concerning (i) state and federal securities laws, "blue-sky" laws; (ii) the provisions of the Employee Retirement Income Security Act of 1974 or any other state or federal pension or employee benefits laws; (iii) federal and state antitrust laws; (iv) federal and state environmental (except as set forth herein), zoning, health and safety, land use, or subdivision laws; (v) federal and state tax laws and regulations (except for our opinion set

APPENDIX 9C   **COMMERCIAL REAL ESTATE TRANSACTIONS**

forth in Section D.10 regarding mortgage taxes); and (vi) federal and state banking laws.

3. Except as expressly provided in Section D.12 above, we express no opinion as to the perfection of any security interests in any items or types of personal property, and no opinion is expressed with respect to (a) the status or condition of title to any property or (b) the priority of any lien or security interest in any collateral held by or available to Lender with respect to any indebtedness or obligation evidenced by or referenced in the Loan Documents.

4. This opinion is limited to the specific opinions expressed herein, and no further opinions are intended to be, or should be, inferred therefrom. This opinion is given as of the date hereof only, and we expressly decline any undertaking or obligation to supplement this opinion or to advise you (a) if any applicable laws change after the date hereof or (b) if we become aware of any facts or in respect to any transactions occurring subsequent to the date hereof, in any case that might change the opinions expressed herein, in whole or in part.

This opinion is rendered only to Lender and the other addressees in connection with the Loan and the Loan Documents, and only with respect to the Loan and the Loan Documents. This opinion may not be relied upon by any addressee for any other purpose, or relied upon by any other person, firm, or entity for any purpose. The addressees may, however, deliver a copy of this opinion to their respective accountants, attorneys, and other professional advisors; to governmental agencies having jurisdiction over an addressee; to any Loan participants; to any transferees of the addressees; to any party servicing the Loan; and to any rating agency involved in the securitization of the Loan, and any such participants, transferees, servicing agents, and rating agencies may rely on this opinion as if it were addressed and delivered to them on the date hereof. Except as set forth above, this opinion may not be duplicated, paraphrased, quoted, summarized, or reproduced in whole or in part.

                                                          Very truly yours,

EXHIBIT A
BORROWER'S CERTIFICATE

EXHIBIT B
SCHEDULE OF SECURITY ACCOUNTS

CHAPTER 10
BASIC RISK ALLOCATION AND INSURANCE CONCEPTS FOR REAL ESTATE TRANSACTIONS

Aaron Johnston, Jr.
Charles E. Comiskey

§ 10.10 OTHER TERMS COMMONLY ENCOUNTERED

[D] Problems with Self-Insurance

[1] Lack of Controlling Law

Page 721, add at end of subsection [1]:

When a deductible is in place, the insurer will defend the policyholder no matter the magnitude of the claim, but pays only for the portion of the loss in excess of the amount of the deductible. Depending on the wording of the policy, the deductible can apply on a per occurrence basis or a per claim basis. In the event of multiple claims arising out of one occurrence, a per claim basis could prove catastrophic to the insured party. A deductible sometimes erodes the policy limit.

[2] Verification of Creditworthiness

Page 721, add at end of subsection [2]:

When a self-insured retention ("SIR") is in place, the insurer will not provide a defense unless the claim exceeds the amount of the SIR and will pay only for the portion of the loss in excess of the amount of the SIR. Depending on the wording of the policy, the SIR can apply on a per occurrence basis or a per claim basis. In the event of multiple claims arising out of one occurrence, a per claim basis could prove catastrophic to the insured party. The full policy limit is usually available in excess of the SIR.

APPENDIX 10B
TENANT'S INSURANCE

Page 725, second column, third row in the table, sixth line, change: "products/completed" *to* "product-completed."

Page 737, add new appendix:

APPENDIX 10G
DEED OF TRUST INSURANCE, INDEMNITY, AND WAIVER PROVISIONS
(MORTGAGEE'S FORM)

1. **INSURANCE.** For so long as the Indebtedness remains outstanding, Grantor will, at Grantor's sole expense, procure and maintain the following insurance coverages:

    (a) Property Insurance.

    (i) **Form.** "Causes of loss—special form" (formerly known as "all risks").

    (ii) **Limit.** Full replacement cost.

    (iii) **Coverage.** All improvements constituting a part of the Mortgaged Property and all furniture, fixtures, and equipment located therein.

    (iv) **Endorsements.**

    (1) Ordinance of law coverage endorsement;

    (2) Standard Mortgagee Clause;

    (3) Flood insurance if the Mortgaged Property is located in a special flood hazard area, as defined in the Flood Disaster Act of 1973.

    (v) **Waiver of Subrogation.** In favor of Lender Parties.

    (b) **Business Income Insurance.** [*Loss of rents equivalent coverage if Grantor is leasing all or a portion of the Mortgaged Property to third parties or business interruption coverage if Grantor is the sole occupant of the Mortgaged Property.*]

    (i) **Limit.** [*Coverage for no less than 12 months of rents if loss of rents equivalent is required or 6 months of income and expenses if business interruption equivalent is required.*]

    (ii) **Waiver of Subrogation.** In favor of Lender Parties.

    (c) **Commercial General Liability Insurance ("CGL").**

    (i) **Form.** ISO CG 0001 1096 or equivalent.

(ii) **Basis.** Occurrence.

(iii) **Limits.** $1,000,000 per occurrence

$2,000,000 general aggregate

$2,000,000 product-completed operations aggregate limit

$1,000,000 personal and advertising injury limit

$ 50,000 damage to premises rented to you limit

$ 5,000 medical expense limit

(iv) **Required Endorsements.**

(1) Aggregate limits of insurance per location;

(2) Lender Parties will be included as "additional insureds" using ISO additional insured form CG 2026 1185, without modification;

(3) A waiver of subrogation in favor of Lender Parties;

(4) A deletion of the contractual claim exclusions for personal injury and advertising injury; and

(5) Severability of interests.

(v) **Other Insurance.** Policy to contain standard CGL "other insurance" wording, unmodified in any way that would make Grantor's coverage excess over or contributory with the additional insured's own commercial general liability coverage.

(vi) **Deductible.** No deductible or self-insured retention in excess of $10,000 to apply to any coverage provided by the CGL policy without the prior written approval of Lender.

(d) **Workers' Compensation and Employer Liability Coverage.**

(i) **Workers' Compensation.** Statutory limits (if state has no statutory limit, $1,000,000).

(ii) **Alternative Forms.** No "alternative" form of coverage shall be accepted.

(iii) **Employer's Liability.** Employer's liability limits: $1,000,000 each accident for bodily injury by accident or $1,000,000 each employee for bodily injury by disease.

(iv) **Waiver of Subrogation.** In favor of Lender Parties

(e) **Business Auto Liability Insurance.**

   (i) **Basis.** Occurrence.

   (ii) **Limit.** $1,000,000 per occurrence.

   (iii) **Required Endorsements.**

   (1) Lender Parties will be included as "additional insureds"; and

   (2) A waiver of subrogation in favor of Lender Parties.

(f) **Umbrella Liability Insurance.**

   (i) **Basis.** Occurrence.

   (ii) **Limit.** $5,000,000 per occurrence.

   $5,000,000 aggregate

   (iii) **Required Endorsements.**

   (1) Aggregate limits of insurance per location;

   (2) Lender Parties will be included as "additional insureds"; and

   (3) To have same date of inception and expiration as CGL policy.

(g) **Other Grantor Insurance Coverage.** Grantor will, at Grantor's sole expense, procure and maintain any other and further insurance coverages that Lender or Lender's lender may require.

(h) **Form of Policies and Additional Requirements.**

   (i) **Insurance Carrier Requirements.** Bests Rating of "A," or better, and Bests Financial Size Category of VIII, or better, and/or *Standard & Poor Insurance Solvency Review* A–, or better. All carriers admitted to engage in the business of insurance in the State or Commonwealth in which the Mortgaged Property is located.

   (ii) **Other Insurance.** All policies must be endorsed to be primary policies of Lender and lender being excess, secondary, and noncontributing.

   (iii) **Notice.** No cancellation, nonrenewal, or material modification without 30 days' prior written notice by insurance carrier to Lender and lender.

(iv) **Aggregate Limits.** Lender must be notified in writing immediately by Grantor of claims against Grantor that might cause a reduction below seventy-five percent (75%) of any aggregate limit of any policy.

(v) **Evidence of Grantor's Insurance.**

(1) Property and business income insurance must be evidenced by ACORD form 27, "Evidence of Property Insurance."

(2) CGL and workers' compensation insurance must be evidenced by ACORD form 25s, "Certificate of Liability Insurance."

(3) Certificate or evidence of insurance must be delivered together with executed Deed of Trust and a new certificate or evidence of insurance must be delivered no later than 30 days prior to expiration of existing policy.

(vi) **Endorsements.** Copies of endorsements must be attached to ACORD forms 25s and 27 delivered to Lender. "Additional insured" or "beneficiary" on endorsements should be "Lender Parties" as defined in Paragraph 2(a) of this Deed of Trust.

2. **INDEMNITIES AND WAIVERS.**

    (a) **Definitions.** For purposes of this Deed of Trust:

    (i) **Grantor Parties.** "Grantor Parties" means (A) Grantor and (B) Grantor's shareholders, members, partners, directors, officers, employees, sublessees, licensees, invitees, agents, and contractors;

    (ii) **Lender Parties.** "Lender Parties" means (A) Lender, (B) Trustee, (C) the shareholders, members, partners, affiliates, and subsidiaries of either Lender or Trustee, and (D) any directors, officers, employees, agents, or contractors of such persons or entities enumerated in (A) through (C);

    (iii) **Indemnify.** "Indemnify" means to protect another party against a Liability and/or to compensate a party for a Liability actually incurred;

    (iv) **Defend.** "Defend" means to oppose a potential or actual Liability on behalf of another party in litigation or other proceeding with counsel reasonably acceptable to Lender and to pay all costs associated with the preparation or prosecution of the defense;

(v) **Waive.** "Waive" means to knowingly and voluntarily relinquish a right and/or release another party from liability in connection with a claim;

(vi) **Liabilities.** "Liabilities" means all liabilities, claims, damages (including consequential damages), losses, penalties, litigation, demands, causes of action (whether in tort or contract, in law or at equity or otherwise), suits, proceedings, judgments, disbursements, charges, assessments, and expenses (including attorneys' and experts' fees and expenses incurred in investigating, defending, or prosecuting any litigation, claim, or proceeding);

(vii) **ISO.** The term "ISO" means Insurance Services Office;

(viii) **Personal Injury, Bodily Injury, and Mortgaged Property Damage.** "Bodily Injury," "Personal Injury," "Mortgaged Property Damage," and "Advertising Injury" will have the same meanings as in the form of commercial general insurance policy CG 0001 1096 issued by ISO. The definitions will not be limited by any exclusions contained in such form; and

(ix) **Grantor's Insurable Injuries.** A "Grantor's Insurable Injury" refers to any of the following:

(1) **Occurrences in the Mortgaged Property.** Any Personal Injury, Bodily Injury, Property Damage, or Advertising Injury whatsoever occurring in the Mortgaged Property;

(2) **Occurrences Outside the Mortgaged Property.** Any Personal Injury, Bodily Injury, or Advertising Injury caused by a Grantor Party and occurring outside the Mortgaged Property; or

(3) **Property Damage.** Any Property Damage suffered by a Grantor Party on the Mortgaged Property.

(b) **Indemnities with Respect to Performance.** To the fullest extent permitted by law, Grantor will Indemnify and Defend Lender Parties against all Liabilities arising out of the following:

(i) **Conduct of Business.** The conduct of Grantor's business;

(ii) **Violation of Applicable Law.** The violation of or failure to comply with, or the alleged violation of or alleged failure to comply with, any Applicable Law by a Grantor Party;

(iii) **Breach of Deed of Trust.** Any breach, violation, or nonperformance of any term, condition, covenant, or other obligation of Grantor under this Deed of Trust or any other Loan Document; or

(iv) **Misrepresentations.** Any misrepresentations made by Grantor or any guarantor of Grantor's obligations in connection with this Deed of Trust or any other Loan Document.

(c) **Indemnities with Respect to Grantor's Insurable Injuries.** To the fullest extent permitted by law, Grantor will Indemnify and Defend Lender Parties against Liabilities arising from Grantor's Insurable Injuries.

(d) **Waiver.** To the fullest extent permitted by law, Grantor, on behalf of all Grantor Parties, Waives all Liabilities against Lender Parties arising from Insurable Risks.

(e) **Scope of Indemnities and Waivers.** The Indemnities, Waivers, and obligations to Defend contained in this Deed of Trust (i) Will be enforced even if the Liability in question is caused by the active or passive negligence or sole, joint, concurrent, or comparative negligence of any of the Lender Parties, and regardless of whether liability without fault or strict liability is imposed or sought to be imposed on any of the Lender Parties, but not to the extent of the percentage of Liabilities that a final judgment of a court of competent jurisdiction establishes under the comparative negligence principles of the State or Commonwealth in which the Mortgaged Property is located, that a Liability was proximately caused by the willful misconduct or gross negligence of that Lender Party (provided, however, that in such event the Indemnity or Waiver will remain valid for all other Lender Parties), (ii) are independent of, and will not be limited by, each other or any insurance obligations in this Deed of Trust (whether or not complied with), and (iii) will survive the expiration or earlier termination of this Deed of Trust until all Liabilities against Lender Parties are fully and finally barred by the applicable statutes of limitations.

[OPTIONAL PROVISIONS]

(f) **Allocation of Risks.** *Lender and Grantor have agreed to allocate risks associated with the injuries described in* Paragraphs 2(c) and 2(d) *to Grantor.*

  (i) **Consideration for Grantor's Indemnities and Waivers.**

   (1) **Lender's Reliance.** *In reliance on the Indemnities and Waivers contained in* Paragraphs 2(c) *and* 2(d) *and the agreement by Grantor to obtain and maintain in force the insurance policies described in* Paragraph 1, *and to obtain in connection with such policies, certain additional insured endorsements, waiver of subrogation endorsements and/or contractual liability coverage for the benefit of the Lender Parties, Lender may elect not to carry primary insurance with respect the risks allocated to Grantor.*

   (2) **Consideration.** *If Lender had been required to carry primary insurance with respect to risks allocated to Grantor, the monetary considerations of this transaction would have been different and the interest rate paid by Grantor for the Mortgaged Property would have been greater or Lender would have required that Grantor reimburse Lender for the premiums incurred by Lender for such primary insurance coverage.*

  (ii) **No Reliance by Grantor.** *Grantor expressly agrees that in order to pay any Liabilities (and, if applicable, costs of Indemnifying and/or Defending Lender Parties) arising from the risks allocated to Grantor, Grantor is not relying upon Lender or Lender's insurance, but rather is relying upon the following:*

   (1) **Grantor's Insurance.** *The insurance policies referenced in Paragraph 1, and any additional insurance Grantor may elect to carry, to the extent the risks allocated to Grantor are covered by such insurance policies;*

*(2) **Grantor's Funds**. Its own funds, to the extent Grantor fails to carry such insurance, to the extent of deductibles or self-insured retentions under insurance policies carried by Grantor, and/or to the extent Liabilities exceed Grantor's insurance limits or are not covered by Grantor's policies; and*

*(3) **Third Parties**. Third parties other than Lender Parties to the extent Liabilities arising out of risks allocated to Grantor are caused by the actions of such third parties.*

CHAPTER 11
ENVIRONMENTAL ISSUES IN COMMERCIAL REAL ESTATE SALES AND LEASES
Jack Fersko

§ 11.02 LAWS IMPOSING ENVIRONMENTAL LIABILITY— GENERALLY

[C] Common Law

Page 743, add to note 5:

See also Z.A.O., Inc. v. Yarbrough Drive Ctr. Joint Venture, 50 S.W.3d 531 (Tex. Ct. App. 2001). Although the Texas Court of Appeals upheld a breach of contract claim under a lease due to contamination of a gas station site by a former tenant, the court determined that an action in trespass cannot be supported when the contaminants existing do not exceed state action levels, and that a nuisance claim cannot be upheld when the proofs do not establish that the discharge was the result of a negligent or intentional encroachment upon the interest of another.

See also Adams v. Cleveland-Cliffs Iron Co., 237 Mich. App. 51, 67, 602 N.W.2d 215, 222 (1999). In a case of first impression for the Michigan courts, the Court of Appeals of Michigan distinguished between trespass and nuisance, holding that to prevail in trespass, a plaintiff must prove an "intrusion of a physical, tangible object" that is not supported by vibrations, noise, dust, and smoke emanating from the defendant's mining operations. Rather, such intangible intrusions would support only a nuisance claim, provided the plaintiff establishes the intrusions were unreasonable and resulted in significant harm.

§ 11.03 THE COMPREHENSIVE ENVIRONMENTAL RESPONSE, COMPENSATION, AND LIABILITY ACT

Page 743, add to note 6:

See generally Commander Oil Corp. v. Barlo Equip. Corp., 215 F.3d 321 (2d Cir. 2000), *cert. denied,* 121 S. Ct. 427, 148 L. Ed. 2d 436 (2000). In a case of first impression before the U.S. Court of Appeals for the Second Circuit, the court faced the issue of whether a lessee/sublessor could be held liable as an "owner" under CERCLA. Although the court determined that "owner" liability should not attach in the matter *sub judice,* the court did conclude that there may, in fact, be circumstances in which "owner" liability should attach to a lessee. In reaching this conclusion, the court pointed to a number of factors that could transform a tenant into an owner for purposes of CERCLA, including (1) the lease term; (2) control over space use; (3) the landlord's inability to terminate a lease prior to the expiration of the lease term; (4) the lessee's right to sublease; (5) the lessee's responsibility for the payment of taxes, insurance, and maintenance costs; and (6) the lessee's responsibility for structural repairs. It is therefore important for a tenant under a long-term lease or a "bond" lease to consider the implications of potential "owner" liability under CERCLA.

Page 744, add to note 10:

See also Carson Harbor Village, Ltd. v. Unocal Corp., 270 F.3d 863, 53 E.R.C. (BNA) 1321 (9th Cir. 2001). In a case of first impression before the United States Court of Appeals for the Ninth Circuit, the court faced the issue of whether passive migration of contamination during a prior owner's period of ownership, constitutes "disposal" under CERCLA, and thereby attaches liability to such interim landowner. The court held that the mere passive migration of soil contamination does not constitute "disposal" under CERCLA. In rendering its decision, the Ninth Circuit sided with a similar conclusion reached by the Second, Third, and Sixth Circuits. *United States v. CDMG Realty Co.*, 96 F.3d 706 (3d Cir. 1996); *ABB Indus. Sys., Inc. v. Prime Tech. Inc.*, 120 F.3d 351 (2d Cir. 1997); *United States v. 150 Acres of Land*, 204 F.3d 698 (6th Cir. 2000). However, the first circuit court to decide this issue, the Fourth Circuit, determined that passive migration of contamination does constitute "disposal" under CERCLA. *Nurad, Inc. v. William E. Hooper & Sons Co.*, 966 F.2d 837 (4th Cir. 1992). Thus, there is a split among the circuit courts, making the issue of whether passive migration of contamination does constitute "disposal" under CERCLA, an issue ripe for resolution by the United States Supreme Court.

Page 745, add to note 18:

See Container Group Inc. v. American Financial Group, Inc., 128 F. Supp. 2d 470 (S.D. Ohio 2001) wherein the court held that a party will lose the "innocent landowner defense" if such party does not establish that they exercised due care concerning the hazardous substance at issue; *Thomson Precision Ball Co. LLC v. PSB Assocs. Liquidating Trust,* 2001 U.S. Dist. LEXIS 340 (D. Conn. 2001) (order denying renewed motion to dismiss). In *Thomson,* the U.S. District Court for the District of Connecticut held that a purchaser of real estate can achieve innocent landowner status even when the purchaser acquires property knowing of contamination. If the purchaser can establish that it did not know or have reason to know of the hazardous substances complained of in the suit, the purchaser is entitled to "partial" innocent landowner status.

§ 11.04 STATE "SUPERFUND" AND LIEN LAWS

Page 746, add to note 21:

Fireman's Fund Ins. Co. v. City of Lodi, 41 F. Supp. 2d (E.D. Cal. 1999), was affirmed in part and reversed and remanded in part by the Ninth Circuit in *Fireman's Fund Ins. Co. v. City of Lodi,* 271 F.3d 911 (9th Cir. 2001). The district court had determined that a municipal hazardous substance law is not preempted by federal law, but abstained from determining whether such law was preempted by state environmental law. The Ninth Circuit determined that the district court erred in abstaining from deciding the issue, and held that hazardous substance cleanup laws of municipalities are not preempted by state law.

Page 747, add to note 25:

See also In re 229 Main St. Ltd. Partnership v. Massachusetts Dept. of Envtl. Protection, 262 F.3d 1 (1st Cir. 2001). In a case of first impression for the circuit courts, the First Circuit held that the automatic stay provision of the Bankruptcy Code does not prevent a state from perfecting its super-priority lien post-petition.

§ 11.06 CONTRACTUAL REALLOCATION OF LIABILITY

Page 750, add to note 31:

See generally Foster v. United States, 130 F. Supp. 2d 68 (D.D.C. 2001). The court determined that the transfer of property in "as is" condition did not result in an assumption of risk for contamination that the buyer did not know of at the time of the transfer.

Page 751, add to note 36:

Waste Management of Alameda County, Inc. v. East Bay Regional Park Dist., 135 F. Supp. 2d 1071 (N.D. Cal. 2001) (in order to shift CERCLA liability, a contract must directly, clearly, and unambiguously address the issue).

Page 751, add new note 39.1 at the end of the last paragraph:

... land and bind successors on title and interest.[39.1]

[39.1] *But see Calabrese v. McHugh*, 170 F. Supp. 2d 243 (D. Conn. 2001), wherein the court determined that an acknowledgement by a grantee within a deed of the grantor's dumping activities, and a covenant within that deed not to sue for such activities, which covenant by its terms was binding on the grantee's successors and assigns, was personal in nature, did not "touch and concern" the land, and was not "appurtenant" to the land. Consequently, the release was not binding upon a subsequent owner of the property that acquired the property without actual knowledge of the deed provision. The court noted that it was not deciding what impact actual knowledge of a subsequent purchaser of the deed provision would have in a future case involving the same facts.

Page 751, add at end of page:

In a decision that will challenge the drafting techniques of, and produce nightmares for, all real estate counsel, the U.S. District Court for the Northern District of Alabama held that a seller of real estate that agreed to remediate contamination "at its sole expense" waived its right to bring a CERCLA contribution action against its predecessor in title and other potentially responsible parties. *Southdown v. Allen,* 119 F. Supp. 2d 1223 (N.D. Ala. 2000). Plaintiffs brought a suit against the predecessor in title, Les Allen ("Allen"), who sold the plaintiffs all of the stock in Allworth, Inc. ("Allworth"). As a result of the stock sale, the plaintiffs acquired Allworth, which owned and operated a hazardous waste recycling facility. All of the issued and outstanding shares of Allworth, in turn, were sold to Nortru, Inc. ("Nortru"), pursuant to a Stock Purchase Agreement ("Stock Agreement").[39.2]

In accordance with the terms of the Stock Agreement, the parties entered into a Remediation Agreement.[39.3] Pursuant to the Remediation Agreement, SETS agreed, "at its sole expense," to remediate all known contamination and all unknown contamination discovered during the cleanup of the known contamination. *Southdown,* 119 F. Supp. 2d at 1226. The Remediation Agreement also included a broad indemnity by SETS, in favor of Nortru, for any loss resulting from its performance or breach of its obligations under the Remediation Agreement. The Stock Agreement contained a broad indemnity in favor of Nortru, in part, for environmental claims relating to the contamination. SETS and SES also agreed within the Stock Agreement to a non-compete provision that stated, in part, that a portion of the value of the stock was attributable to the business relationship with Allworth's customers.

After Southdown filed suit, it amended its complaint to name certain current and former customers of Allworth. Allen responded to the complaint by filing a third-party complaint against Allworth and Nortru and a cross-claim against the current and former Allworth customers. The current and former Allworth customers, in turn, filed an action against additional current and former customers of Allworth. Nortru and Allworth filed a motion for partial summary judgment, and Southdown cross-moved for summary judgment. Allen and the third-party defendants joined in the Nortru and Allworth motion.

The central issue before the court was whether Southdown was barred from pursuing any cost recovery claim, since the Remediation Agreement provided for the cleanup to be performed at Southdown's "sole expense." Southdown argued that the contract provision was intended only to address the respective liability of the contracting parties. Nortru and Allworth, however, argued that the term "sole expense" meant that only Southdown would pay for the remediation.

Applying Texas law, the court determined that the words "sole expense" were clear on their face. Consequently, the court would not allow parole evidence to establish that the term "sole expense" should be limited in application to the contracting parties, rather than being extended to those who are not a party to the Remediation Agreement. The decision reflects the court's clear desire to preserve the integrity of the business acquisition. Because the suit resulted in claims against the Allworth customers, which could materially interfere with the business relationship with those customers, the court reasoned that the suit violated the covenant not to compete. Also, because of the broad indemnifications set forth in the agreements, the suit would only come full circle back to Southdown, since Nortru could advance a claim for indemnification inasmuch as the suit against Nortru related to the environmental conditions with respect to which Southdown provided an indemnity.

In reaching its decision, the court circumvented the express language of the agreements, which provided that the agreements were not intended to benefit anyone other than the contracting parties. As such, Southdown argued that neither Allen nor the Allworth customers should benefit from the cleanup obligation undertaken by Southdown in the agreements. The court determined that under Texas law a contract can incidentally benefit a person that is not a party to, and cannot enforce, a contract. Employing that logic, the court concluded that a contract can also benefit a third party even when the contracting parties did not intend to confer a benefit upon such third party. Consequently, the court allowed Allen and the current and former customers of Allworth to rely upon the contract language in order to avoid liability to Southdown.

Finally, the court determined that by using the "sole expense" language, Southdown expressly waived its right to contribution against Allen and the Allworth customers under CERCLA. According to the court, the only way for Southdown to have retained the right to sue others was for Southdown to have expressly retained its right to sue for contribution under CERCLA.

As a result of the *Southdown* decision, when a seller, buyer, landlord, or tenant undertakes to remediate a site, it should not use terms such as "at the expense of " or "at the sole cost or expense of " or similar language. Rather, the party agreeing to cleanup should express the obligation by providing that the remediation will be performed "at no cost or expense" to the other contracting party. In addition, and in order to be perfectly secure in light of the *Southdown* decision, it is recommended that the obligor expressly reserve the right to bring any claims it may have against others by way of contribution, indemnification, or otherwise, under common law or statute, regardless of whether the claim or cause of action now exists or is subsequently created or enacted. On the other hand, the beneficiary of such cleanup obligation should consider addressing expressly the issue of indemnification by the obligor in the event the beneficiary is brought into the action as a responsible party by virtue of its present owner or operator status.

[39.2] The plaintiffs in the action are Southdown, Inc., and Southdown Environmental LLC ("SELLC"). The Stock Agreement was entered into by Southdown Environmental Treatment Systems, Inc. ("SETS"), and Southdown Environmental Systems, Inc. ("SES"). Southdown, Inc., guaranteed the obligations of SETS and SES. SETS merged into SELLC.

ENVIRONMENTAL ISSUES § 11.11[B]

The court referred to all of the plaintiffs as "Southdown," and the plaintiffs will be referred to herein in the same manner.

[39.3] The Remediation Agreement was entered into only by SETS. Southdown, Inc., guaranteed the obligations of SETS.

§ 11.09 DISCLOSURE AND TRANSACTION-TRIGGERED LAWS

Page 780, add after second paragraph:

It is important that real estate counsel recognize that a disclosure obligation may also arise from non-environmental statutes. For example, in New Jersey, the legislature adopted the New Residential Construction Off-Site Conditions Disclosure Act ("Disclosure Act"), N.J. Stat. Ann. § 46:3C-1 to -12, which limits the disclosure obligation of a seller of new residential construction. However, in *Nobrega v. Edison Glen Associates,* 327 N.J. Super. 415 (App. Div.), *cert. granted,* 165 N.J. 137 (2000), the appellate court held that although a developer may comply with the Disclosure Act, liability for failing to disclose off-site environmental conditions can attach under the state's Consumer Fraud Act, N.J. Stat. Ann. § 56:8-1 to -20. *Nobrega v. Edison Glenn Assocs.*, 327 N.J. Super. 415 (App. Div. 2000), was modified and remanded to the trial court by the New Jersey Supreme Court. *Nobrega v. Edison Glenn Assocs.*, 167 N.J. 520 (2001). The court determined that the Disclosure Act prospectively precluded purchasers of newly constructed residential real estate from suing under the State's Consumer Fraud Act.

Page 781, add to note 66:

Hawaii Environmental Disclosure Law, Haw. Rev. Stat. Ann. §§ 343D-1 to -11, repealed June 14, 2001, by Act 247, 2001 Haw. Sess. Laws; Illinois Responsible Property Transfer Act of 1988 ch. 765, Ill. Comp. Stat. Ann. §§ 90/1-90/7, repealed Aug. 9, 2001, by P.A. 92-0299.

§ 11.11 LANDLORD AND TENANT ISSUES

[B] Environmental Compliance Issues

Page 794, add new note 72.1 at end of third sentence of the second full paragraph:

. . . is being used and maintained in compliance with environmental laws.[72.1]

[72.1] *See New York v. Green*, 96 N.Y.2d 403, 754 N.E.2d 179, 729 N.Y.S.2d 420 (Ct. App. 2001) wherein the court determined that a landlord is liable for the activities of its tenants resulting in a discharge of contaminants on the landlord's property when the landlord has control over the activities of the tenant and has reason to believe the tenant will be using contaminants on the rental property.

Page 795, add new note 73.1 at end of first sentence of the first full paragraph:

. . . until all environmental activities are completed.[73.1]

[73.1] *But see River Road Assocs. v. Chesapeake Display and Packaging Co., Inc.*, 104 F. Supp. 2d 418 (D.N.J. 2000), wherein the court determined that a provision in a lease permitting the landlord to reinstate the lease upon its expiration if the tenant fails to return the leasehold in a condition required by the lease terms is an unenforceable penalty.

Page 795, add new note 73.2 at end of second sentence of the first full paragraph:

. . . with the environmental requirements of the lease.[73.2]

[73.2] *See NRC Corp. v. Amoco Oil Co.*, 205 F.3d 1007 (7th Cir. 2000), wherein the court held that, on the basis of the broad lease indemnity, the tenant was liable to the landlord for loss of the use of property owned by the landlord and contiguous to the leasehold estate, even though the contamination did not migrate beyond the leasehold estate.

§ 11.12 ENVIRONMENTAL RISK INSURANCE

Page 806, add at end of section:*

An environmental insurance policy is written for a term of years, and a one-time premium is paid when the policy is issued. Although the per square foot cost of a policy, when amortized over the life of a policy, may be small, there is nevertheless a significant up-front capital expenditure. Other than contractor's pollution legal liability insurance, which is available on an "occurrence" basis, most types of coverage are written on a "claims made" basis. As such, coverage will be available only for a claim made and reported to the carrier during the policy period, or in some

---

*Sections [A] through [E] were adapted from an article by the author and Ann M. Waeger, Esq., initially presented in *The ACREL Papers—Fall 2000,* published by the American Law Institute American Bar Association, titled "The Emerging Role of Environmental Insurance in Commercial Real Estate Transactions: Issues and Answers."

instances during an extended reporting period. It is therefore important to evaluate properly the length of the policy term when acquiring an environmental insurance policy.

[A] Types of Coverage

The increased demand for environmental insurance has resulted in a tremendous growth in the various forms of environmental insurance coverage now available in the market. Although some carriers limit the number of types of policies they issue, others are continuing to expand on their offerings, showing an ever-increasing degree of creativity to meet the market's growing demand.

This section will focus on the main environmental insurance coverage offerings—namely, pollution legal liability insurance, cost overrun insurance, brownfield insurance, and secured creditor insurance. Insurance carriers refer to these forms of coverage by different names, and some offer variations on the same theme, depending on the risk involved. There are also many additional types of environmental insurance policies available. They include:

- Storage tank pollution liability insurance
- Closure and post-closure care insurance
- Contractor's pollution liability insurance
- General contractor's pollution liability insurance
- Professional pollution liability insurance
- Commercial general liability insurance with contractor's pollution and professional liability insurance
- Commercial general liability insurance with pollution liability insurance
- Marina pollution liability insurance
- Agribusiness pollution liability insurance
- Dealer and repair pollution liability insurance
- Portfolio pollution liability insurance
- Asbestos pollution liability insurance
- Lead abatement contractors pollution liability insurance

[B] Pollution Legal Liability Insurance

Pollution legal liability insurance is the generic designation for the type of insurance issued by all insurance carriers that is designed to provide coverage for on-site cleanup costs, claims for off-site cleanup costs, and claims for on-site and off-site bodily injury and property damage resulting from a pollution incident. This type of insurance also includes legal defense costs (which will be both subject to and deducted from policy limits) and may include business interruption and extra expense coverage, as well as diminution in property value due to a pollution incident. Coverage is available for preexisting and new conditions on a site, and depending on site conditions, coverage may be available for known conditions (for example, where contamination has been left in place with government permission and is being controlled by way of engineering controls, such as a cap).

Some insurance carriers have multiple policies for this generic type of coverage. Which policy the carrier will issue depends on the risk involved in the particular transaction and the coverage desired by the insured. For example, Gulf Insurance Company offers a policy entitled "Property Owner's Policy" and a policy entitled "Pollution Legal Liability Policy"; Zurich Insurance Company offers policies entitled "Real Estate Environmental Liability Insurance," "Environmental Cleanup and Liability Insurance," and "Environmental Impairment Liability Insurance"; AIG Environmental offers a policy entitled "Commercial Pollution Legal Liability" and a policy entitled "Commercial Real Estate Pollution Legal Liability"; and Kemper Environmental Ltd. offers policies entitled "Environmental Response, Compensation and Liability Insurance," "Environmental Liability Insurance," and "Environmental Insurance for Real Property Transfer." These policies differ in that some are designed for low-risk properties (such as office buildings) and provide broader coverage, by way of either a more expansive insuring agreement or fewer policy exclusions, while others are designed for medium- or high-risk properties (such as manufacturing facilities) and provide a narrower scope of coverage.

Each of the insurance carriers has its own set of minimums with respect to policy deductibles, but by way of a broad generalization, policy deductibles range from $5,000 to $10,000. Likewise, policies can be written for a term of up to 10 years and policy limits of up to $100 million per occurrence and $200 million in the aggregate. Most insurance carriers will require a Phase I site assessment before issuing a policy, although in certain situations additional site investigation may be required. Some insurance carriers will require only a database search and a transaction screen before issuing a policy. The deductible, amount of coverage, term of coverage, site conditions, and surrounding site conditions will all influence the policy premium.

Some insurance carriers will provide pollution legal liability protection for portfolios of real estate under a single policy. This provides the real estate investor the benefit of negotiating only one policy. There are a number of issues that must be addressed, however, when negotiating a portfolio-type policy, including the conditions under which newly acquired properties can be added to the policy and the cost for adding newly acquired properties to the policy.

[C] Cost Overrun Insurance

Cost overrun insurance, which is also known as stop gap, cleanup cap, cleanup cost containment, and remediation stop loss insurance, is designed to cover an increase in the cost of a known cleanup due to cost overruns. Typically, cost overrun insurance is issued when a policyholder has completed a site investigation and has received an approval from a governmental authority of its remedial action plan. Today, however, many insurance carriers have their own risk control groups and will issue coverage if their risk control group is satisfied with the cleanup plan.

A critical issue that must be examined when negotiating a cost overrun policy is what events and circumstances will be covered as "cost overruns." For example, will the policy cover the increase in the cost of a cleanup if the increase is due to the following events or conditions:

- Higher concentrations of contaminants already noted in the cleanup plan,
- The broader presence of known contaminants,
- Newly discovered contamination within or outside of already identified areas of concern,
- Broader cleanup requirements due to a change in regulatory requirements,
- Failure of a cleanup plan,
- Failure of a cleanup system,
- Negligence of the environmental consultant, or
- Unexpected geological conditions?

Depending on the insurance carrier, policy limits for cost overrun insurance can be as high as $100 million per occurrence and $200 million in the aggregate, and policies can be written for a term of 1 to 10 years, and possibly longer if an insurer can obtain reinsurance for the risk. These policies are written on a "claims made" basis. Consequently, when determining a policy term, an insured must consider whether the site will be the subject of a development and whether part of the development (such as improvements to be built) will serve as an engineering control in connection with the cleanup, thereby requiring the insured to account for the time period for obtaining development approvals and constructing the improvements. Notwithstanding the policy term, cost overrun coverage normally will end when a No Further Action Letter is issued for the cleanup (if that takes place prior to the expiration of the policy term). It is important that the policy be negotiated so that post–No Further Action Letter requirements (such as continued monitoring) are covered. In addition, the cost overrun policy will contain a self-insured retention, which normally will equal the estimated cost of a cleanup plus a multiple (10 or 20 percent) of the estimated cost of cleanup. Policy premiums generally will be a percentage of the estimated cost of cleanup, although the setting of the premium will be affected by the limits of liability, the self-insured retention, the nature and anticipated duration of the cleanup, and the remediation contractor.

There is an increasing trend today for environmental cleanup contractors to quote fixed-price cleanups. This phenomenon is a result of the increased competition between environmental remediation contractors and the fact that the industry has gained greater experience in the nature of cleanups and the unknowns typically encountered during cleanups. To protect themselves, however, and at the same time provide a comfort level to the property owner, such contractors in many instances purchase cost overrun insurance.

[D] Brownfield Insurance

Brownfield insurance is a policy that combines both pollution legal liability insurance and cost overrun insurance into one policy. A brownfield type of policy is the preferred choice where an insured is redeveloping a site on which a cleanup must be performed. The insured can better protect against a gap in coverage that easily can result if two different policies must be negotiated, with potentially two different sets of definitions, exclusions, and conditions.

[E] Secured Creditor Insurance

Secured creditor insurance is a relatively new environmental insurance product. Although much of the lending community's concern for environmental liability was addressed by the federal and state governments with the enactment of a variety of lender liability protections, the lending community still has had concerns over environmental issues and their potential impact on a credit facility. These concerns relate to questions regarding the borrower's ability to meet its debt service obligations if faced with a costly cleanup during the life of a loan and the lender's ability to realize the full value from its collateral if the collateral is tainted by environmental contamination.

Depending on the insurance carrier issuing the policy, coverage under the secured creditor policy can be as high as $100 million per occurrence and $200 million in the aggregate, and the policy term can be as long as 20 years. Again depending on the insurance carrier, the policy can be written to cover first-party cleanup costs, claims for third-party cleanup costs, claims for third-party bodily injury and property damage, legal defense costs, and payment of the outstanding loan balance. Typically, a secured creditor policy has been written to cover the lesser of the loan balance (provided there was a default under the loan) or cleanup costs (provided there was a foreclosure). Now, however, coverage is available to recover the loan balance after default if there has been a pollution condition at the collateralized property.

Generally, the insurance carriers will issue secured creditor policies based on a transaction screen and a database search, although a Phase I site investigation may be required depending on the size of the loan and the operations conducted on the secured property. Insurance carriers are also providing such coverage on a portfolio basis, so that a lender can add properties to the policy as new loans are closed. In addition, insurance carriers are marketing the insurance as an alternative to a Phase I site assessment. The coverage can be bound faster than the time period normally required to perform a Phase I site investigation, and the cost of the coverage is less than the cost for a Phase I site investigation. As a result, the borrower can save money and close the loan sooner than where a lender requires a Phase I site assessment.

Secured creditor policies have become particularly important in securitized loan transactions. Certain rating agencies, such as Fitch IBCA and Moody's Investors Service, will give additional credit support to commercial mortgaged-backed securities pools that use environmental insurance.

[F] Policy Exclusions*

The insuring agreement section of a policy sets forth the coverage that will be afforded by a policy. The exclusion section of a policy, however, is the heart of the policy, for it is here that the insurance carrier narrows and removes coverage ostensibly afforded by the insuring agreement. Consequently, the exclusions must be examined with utmost care.

In a decision involving a contemporary environmental insurance policy, the United States District Court for the Eastern District of Pennsylvania, in *Goldenberg Development Corp., et al. v. Reliance Insurance Co., for Illinois*, No. 00-CV-3055, 2001 U.S. Dist. LEXIS 12870 (E.D. Pa. 2001), interpreted a policy exclusion, namely, the known conditions exclusion. The court determined that the disclosure of environmental reports does not constitute disclosure of "facts" for purposes of the known conditions exclusion. Prior to this decision, the critical issue that frequently arose in the context of the known conditions exclusion concerned what constituted a known condition and whose knowledge was relevant in determining what conditions would be deemed known conditions. However, maybe even more important now, is the manner in which the insured discloses those conditions that are in fact known to the insured prior to the policy inception.

This decision brings to a head a difficult issue facing prospective insureds. Insurers expect and require an insured to disclose all material facts known to the insured prior to the inception of a policy. However, it is now arguable that the insured undertake the obligation of reviewing and summarizing all environmental conditions disclosed in all known environmental reports.

Frequently, real estate counsel's involvement in the environmental insurance policy process follows the application stage. However, because disclosure of a known condition must be made during the application process, this decision now makes it incumbent upon real estate counsel to review the application and environmental reports filed with the carrier, and examine closely with the client and its environmental consultant, the environmental conditions known to exist at the subject property, to ensure that full and proper disclosure of all material facts was made by the

---

*This section was adapted from an article by the author initially presented in *ACREL News*, Vol. 19, No. 4 (Dec. 2001).

insured during the application process. Alternatively, if the quantity of environmental reports makes this task impracticable, then real estate counsel must negotiate a provision in the policy, that will deem disclosed all conditions identified in documents delivered to the insurer prior to the policy inception, and must require that a list of such documents be appended to the policy.

Chapter 12
INDUSTRIAL LEASES
Philip D. Weller

Page 849, add new section:

§ 12.15 CONDEMNATION AND CASUALTY PROVISIONS THAT SHIFT RISK TO THE TENANT

In drafting industrial leases that the lending community will treat (and price) as being completely "bondable," it may be necessary to include a provision that effectively shifts most of the risk of a casualty or condemnation loss to the tenant. The lender's reasoning is that it is relying primarily on the credit of the tenant in providing the financing—in fact, such financing may be more properly considered an unsecured credit loan to the tenant than a secured mortgage loan to the landlord/developer. Accordingly, the lender wishes the lease to be "bondable" in the sense that the rent stream under the lease will be paid as reliably as interest and principal would be payable on a bond issued by the tenant. While the typical limitations on landlord's remedies in many states, of course, have an impact on the lender's evaluation of the credit risk (*see* **§ 12.11** in the main volume), the typical casualty and condemnation loss provisions will give the lender greater problems in this type of financing transaction. *See* **Forms 12-12** and **12-22** in the main volume for typical casualty and taking/condemnation provisions. The reason that casualty and condemnation provisions are of greater concern in this regard is that they arise from events beyond the control of the landlord or tenant—the risk that the tenant will not pay the rent is essentially the same credit risk as nonpayment of principal or interest. The more typical lease allocation of risk in the case of a casualty or condemnation places much of the economic burden on the landlord, rather than on the tenant, where the lender wishes it to be placed.

Form 12-24, this supplement, reflects an alternate condemnation and casualty provision that effectively shifts the risk of a casualty or condemnation loss to the tenant. Basically, the form obligates the tenant to either restore or irrevocably offer to acquire the landlord's interest in the premises remaining after the taking or casualty for a purchase price that, when coupled with the attendant casualty insurance proceeds or condemnation award, is at least sufficient to pay the outstanding balance of the financing secured by the property. This is often accomplished by attaching a schedule to the lease, very similar in form to an amortization schedule, which lists specified termination dates and provides for the payment on those dates of an amount, a "termination value," sufficient to pay at least the outstanding balance of financing in full. If the landlord has contributed a significant amount of equity to the project, the schedule for the termination values should also, from the landlord's perspective, be negotiated so as to provide for the return of as much of the unamortized equity as possible. In a build-to-suit situation, the goals of the lender and the landlord can also be readily achieved by tying the termination values to the cost of the facility, with appropriate amortization over the term of the lease. A note of caution: The tenant's desire to treat the lease as a true lease for tax and accounting purposes can be impacted depending on the length of the term and the extent that risk of loss is placed on the tenant, and advice of tax counsel should be sought in connection with such provisions to be sure that the desired treatment of the lease, from both the landlord's and the tenant's perspectives, is achieved.

FORM 12-24
CONDEMNATION AND CASUALTY DAMAGE PROVISION— ENTIRE RISK SHIFTED TO TENANT

§ ____ *Condemnation and Casualty.*

(a) Tenant hereby assigns to Landlord any award, compensation, insurance proceeds, or other payment to which Tenant may become entitled by reason of its interest in the Premises other than any award, compensation, or insurance payment made to Tenant for interruption or loss of business, for moving expenses, or for any inventory, machinery, equipment, or other personal property belonging to Tenant, including, without limitation, Tenant's equipment (hereinafter referred to as *"Tenant's Loss"*) by reason of (1) damage to or destruction of the Premises by fire or other casualty or cause (a *"Casualty"*), or (2) any condemnation, requisition, or other taking or sale of the use, occupancy, or title to the Premises or any portion thereof in, by, or on account of any actual or threatened eminent domain proceeding or other action by any governmental authority or other person having the power of eminent domain (a *"Condemnation"*). Tenant is hereby authorized and empowered, at its sole cost and expense, in the name and on behalf of Landlord, Tenant, or otherwise, to appear in any such proceeding or other action; to negotiate, accept, and

INDUSTRIAL LEASES § 12.15

prosecute any claim for any award, compensation, insurance proceeds, or other payment on account of any such casualty or condemnation; and to cause any such award, compensation, insurance proceeds, or other payments to be paid to Landlord, except that Tenant shall be entitled to submit a separate claim for Tenant's Loss and receive and retain any award applicable thereto. All amounts so paid or payable to Landlord or Tenant shall be retained or paid over to the party entitled thereto in accordance with the provisions of this Section. Tenant shall take all appropriate action in connection with each such claim, proceeding, or other action. Landlord and Landlord's Mortgagee *[Note: see **Form 12-18**, in the main volume, for a definition of **"Landlord's Mortgagee"**]* may participate in such proceedings, and Tenant shall deliver all instruments reasonably requested by Landlord or Landlord's Mortgagee to permit such participation, and shall pay all costs and expenses reasonably incurred in connection therewith.

(b) If less than substantially all of the Premises shall be damaged or destroyed by Casualty, or Condemned, then Tenant shall give prompt written notice thereof to Landlord, and this Lease shall continue in full force and effect, and Tenant shall proceed at Tenant's own cost and expense and in conformity with the requirements set forth in Section _____ [reference section dealing with repairs and alterations] with reasonable diligence and promptness to carry out any necessary demolition and to restore, repair, replace, and/or rebuild the Premises in order to restore the Premises, as nearly as practicable, to substantially the same condition, design, and construction as that which existed immediately prior to such Casualty and Condemnation.

(c) Base Rent shall not abate hereunder by reason of any such Casualty or Condemnation, and Tenant shall continue to perform and fulfill all of Tenant's obligations, covenants, and agreements hereunder notwithstanding the same.

(d) Landlord and Tenant shall agree on the maximum cost of such restoration, repair, replacement, or rebuilding, such agreement not to be unreasonably withheld or delayed, and such cost shall be paid first out of Tenant's own funds to the extent such cost exceeds (1) in the case of a Casualty, the net insurance proceeds payable in respect thereof, or (2) in the case of a Condemnation, the net award payable in respect thereof (in either case, the **"Net Award"**), and then out of the Net Award. If Landlord and Tenant cannot agree on the maximum cost of such restoration, repair, replacement, or rebuilding, the issue shall be submitted to arbitration in accordance with the Commercial Arbitration Rules of the American Arbitration Association, on an expedited basis (**"Arbitration"**). The Net Award shall be made available to Tenant for restoration, repair, and rebuilding as follows: (i) if the Net Award does not exceed $_____ (the **"Alteration Cost Threshold"**), and provided that no Event of Default has occurred and is continuing, then the Net Award shall be paid to Tenant (and to the extent the Net Award was previously assigned to Landlord, it will be remitted by Landlord to Tenant) to be applied to the repair and rebuilding work required by this Section, or (ii) if the Net Award exceeds the Alteration Cost Threshold, the proceeds shall be disbursed in accordance with Subsection (g) below.

(e) If at any time during the Term, Tenant shall reasonably determine that all or substantially all of the Premises have been destroyed by Casualty, or all or substantially all of the Premises have been taken by Condemnation, or after any substantial Condemnation of the Premises if the Premises are unsuitable for continued use in Tenant's business, Tenant shall notify Landlord of such event in writing within thirty (30) days of such Condemnation or Casualty. In such event Tenant may either (1) rebuild and/or restore the Premises at Tenant's own cost and expense and in accordance with the requirements set forth herein, or (2) give written notice to Landlord within ninety (90) days after such Condemnation or Casualty of Tenant's intention to terminate this Lease in conformity with the requirements set forth herein. Substantially all of the Premises shall be deemed to have been taken by Condemnation if the remaining portion shall not be of sufficient size or character to permit the operation by Tenant on an economically feasible basis of the business conducted thereon immediately prior to the Condemnation, assuming that such remaining portion had been repaired and restored to the fullest extent possible. Substantially all of the Premises shall be deemed to have been destroyed by Casualty, if, as to any one occurrence, _____ percent (___%) or more of the total net rentable square foot area within the Premises shall be damaged or destroyed and Tenant determines in its reasonable discretion that the Premises are no longer suitable for use in its business. Tenant's notice to Landlord of Tenant's intent to terminate this Lease shall: (A) contain a brief description of the relevant Condemnation or Casualty; (B) specify a date for the termination of this Lease, which shall be the last day of a calendar month not less than 90 nor more than 120 days after such notice is given (the *"Termination Date"*); (C) if such notice of termination shall be based on a reasonable determination by Tenant that after such Casualty or Condemnation the Premises are no longer suitable for use in Tenant's business as aforesaid, contain a certification by Tenant that Tenant will discontinue the use of the Premises in Tenant's ordinary course of business; (D) contain the irrevocable offer of Tenant to purchase Landlord's interest in the Premises (and in the Net Award) on such Termination Date at the Termination Value (defined as the amount specified opposite the applicable Termination Date on Schedule ____ hereto *[Note: see comments in § 12.15, this supplement, for a description of this schedule])*; and (E) contain a commitment by Tenant to deposit with a Depository (defined below) not later than 90 days after the date of the Condemnation or Casualty (but not later than the Termination Date) as security for payment of the purchase price for the Premises the applicable Termination Value less the amount of any Net Award previously paid with respect to such Casualty or Condemnation and held by Landlord or Landlord's designee pursuant to this Section. If Landlord shall reject such offer to purchase by notice (countersigned by Landlord's Mortgagee) given to Tenant not later than thirty (30) days prior to such Termination Date, then this Lease shall terminate on such Termination Date and the Net Award shall be paid and belong to Landlord, plus an amount equal to the deductible payable under the policy or policies of insurance, which shall be paid by Tenant to Landlord. Unless Landlord shall reject such offer to purchase as provided in the preceding sentence, Landlord shall be conclusively deemed to have accepted such offer, and on such Termination Date Landlord shall transfer, and Tenant shall purchase, Landlord's interest in the Premises (and in the Net Award) and upon payment of the purchase price, Tenant's obligation to pay Base Rent shall terminate on the Termination Date. The additional amount, if any, deposited by Tenant pursuant to clause (E) preceding and not applied towards the purchase price of the Premises shall be paid to Tenant on the Termination Date provided that there is no Event of Default then existing. On the Termination Date Landlord shall execute a special warranty deed conveying to Tenant Landlord's interest in the Premises free and clear of all claims and encumbrances except those (excluding any liens) that encumber the Premises on the date hereof or are hereafter placed thereon by Landlord and that do not materially affect the use of the Premises contemplated by this Lease, and Tenant shall pay to Landlord the purchase price therefor.

(f) If, following a Casualty or Condemnation, Tenant shall not give notice of its intention to terminate this Lease in accordance with Subsection (e) above or shall not be entitled to give notice of its intention to terminate this Lease, then this Lease shall continue in full force and effect.

(g) If the Net Award shall exceed the Alteration Cost Threshold, or if an Event of Default has occurred and is continuing, then:

(1) The full amount of the Net Award shall be paid to a depository (the *"Depository"*) to be selected as hereinafter provided. The Depository shall be Landlord's Mortgagee, or if there is no Landlord's Mortgagee, then the Depository shall be a bank or trust company selected by Landlord and approved by Tenant (so long as an Event of Default does not exist under this Lease) which approval shall not be unreasonably withheld or delayed. The Depository shall have no affirmative obligation to prosecute a determination of the amount of, or to effect the collection of, any insurance proceeds or condemnation award or awards, unless the Depository shall have been given an express written undertaking to do so by Landlord and Tenant. Moneys received by the Depository pursuant to the provisions of this Lease shall not be commingled with other funds and shall be held by the Depository in trust, either separately or with other trust funds, for the uses and purposes provided in this Lease. The Depository shall place any moneys held by it into an interest bearing account, and the interest paid or received by the Depository on the moneys so held in trust shall be added to the moneys so held in trust. The Depository shall not be liable or accountable for any

action taken or suffered by the Depository or for any disbursement of moneys made by the Depository in good faith in reliance on advice of legal counsel. In disbursing moneys pursuant to Subsections (g)(2), (g)(3), and (g)(4) below, the Depository may rely conclusively on the information contained in any notice given to the Depository by Tenant in accordance with the provisions of such provision, unless Landlord shall notify the Depository in writing within five (5) business days after the giving of any such notice that Landlord intends to dispute such information, in which case the disputed amount shall not be disbursed but shall continue to be held by the Depository until such dispute shall have been resolved by agreement of the parties or by Arbitration;

(2) Provided that no Event of Default has occurred and is continuing, from time to time, but not more than once in any thirty (30) day period, Tenant may request reimbursement out of the Net Award for the actual costs and expenses incurred by Tenant in connection with such repair and rebuilding. Such requests shall be made by written notice to the Depository, with a copy to Landlord, setting forth in reasonable detail all of such costs and expenses incurred by Tenant. If Landlord shall in good faith desire to dispute the information contained in any such notice given by Tenant, Landlord shall so notify Tenant and the Depository in writing within five (5) business days after the giving of such notice, specifying the amount intended to be disputed and the nature of the dispute. After such five (5) business day period has elapsed, if Landlord has not disputed the information contained in Tenant's Notice, the Depository shall promptly disburse to Tenant out of the Net Award the amount of such costs and expenses. If Landlord disputes the information contained in Tenant's Notice, such dispute shall be resolved by agreement of the parties or by Arbitration, and any undisputed amount shall be released to Tenant;

(3) Upon the completion of such repair and rebuilding, any remaining Net Award shall be paid to and belong to Tenant; and

(4) Notwithstanding any other provision to the contrary contained in this Section, in the event of a temporary Condemnation, this Lease shall remain in full force and effect and Tenant shall be entitled to the Net Award allocable to such temporary Condemnation; except that such portion of the Net Award allocable to the time period after the expiration or termination of the Term of this Lease shall be paid to Landlord.

CHAPTER 14
OFFICE LEASES

§ 14.02 THE OFFICE TENANT'S QUESTIONS

Page 899, add new paragraph at end of section:

A very strong tenant may have a wish list in its request for proposal that is instructive for—but definitely not always applicable to—a smaller tenant. Depending upon the marketplace, the strong tenant may not be able to get all these agreements. In some markets, a smaller tenant may be able to get some of them. A very desirable tenant would like:

1. With regard to the premises:
   (a) continuing rights of first refusal at the rental rate at the time the space is added in adjacent space including space on the same floor and floors above or below the premises, and perhaps on all space in the building;
   (b) expansion options on adjacent space including space on the same floor and floors above or below the premises, and perhaps on all space in the building;
   (c) storage space.
2. With regard to the term:
   (a) a term and rent commencement date based upon substantial completion of the premises, exterior areas, and areas and service facilities (such as air conditioning and elevators), as evidenced by a certificate of occupancy and architect's certificate of completion, advance notice of substantial completion, and an opportunity to inspect the premises and verify the operability of the systems;
   (b) a delay of term and rent commencement for *force majeure*, or any act attributable to the landlord or its contractors including slow response to changes and repair of non-conforming work;

- (c) cancellation rights based upon the payment of, for example, six month's rent;
- (d) numerous renewal options at fixed or indexed rental rates (but not market which may be too high);
- (e) parking, both reserved and unreserved, at fixed or bargain rates, at a higher ratio of spaces to premises area than the landlord usually offers, at convenient locations designated by the tenant.

3. With respect to operating expenses:
   - (a) a gross up of operating expenses to 100 percent;
   - (b) "caps" on operating expenses increases;
   - (c) audit rights with a right to charge the landlord for the cost of the audit if an error is found;
   - (d) numerous exclusions from operating expenses such as those set forth in § **14.10[B][2]**, main volume;
   - (e) no charge (or a fixed or bargain rate) for after-hours HVAC usage.

4. With regard to tenant improvements:
   - (a) an allowance that covers all construction, permitting, and design costs;
   - (b) base building (that is, the landlord's work) that includes access to supplemental power if the tenant's floor is inadequate, telephone and other communication wiring, access to the landlord's emergency generators and fuel (or space at no cost for the tenant's own emergency generator and fuel supply), life support and security systems, adequate cooling, and other legal requirements such as ADA compliance;
   - (c) the tenant's free choice of architect, contractor, and subcontractors;
   - (d) the tenant's right to apply the allowance as it wishes (including as a credit against rent);
   - (e) the tenant's right to require the landlord's contractor to do the work, and no fee to the landlord for supervision in any case, in which event the tenant participates in the bidding (to at least three contractors and major subcontractors) and selection;
   - (f) free parking for the tenant's architect, contractor, and subcontractors during construction;
   - (g) free use of hoists, elevators, utilities and HVAC, loading docks;

OFFICE LEASES § 14.02

    (h) reserved elevators for the weekend when the tenant moves its personal property.
5. With regard to the building:
    (a) HVAC, electrical power, and janitorial service (with a right to do its own for a reduction of operating expenses attributable to janitorial), according to the tenant's specifications;
    (b) services during the tenant's business hours and a limitation of the building "holidays";
    (c) security services;
    (d) access to the premises (and parking lot) at all times, the right to use stairwells between adjoining floors of the premises, and dedicated elevators;
    (e) telecommunications antenna;
    (f) free or bargain rate use of the building amenities (such as health club);
    (g) building identity (that is signage) or at least a restriction of other's signage (such as competitors), lobby, directory, elevator, and floor signage;
    (h) professional building management consistent with the quality of the building;
    (i) the landlord's representation regarding the absence of hazardous material and its promise to remediate at no cost to the tenant any that appears;
    (j) the landlord's representation regarding the compliance with all laws (including ADA, OSHA, and building codes) and its promise to comply with them at no cost to the tenant.
6. Unrestricted right of assignment or sublease without recapture or profit sharing.
7. Unrestricted, or minimally restricted, right to make alterations to the premises.
8. A waiver of the security deposit and any landlord's lien.
9. Rent abatement for interruption of services.
10. The tenant's right to any part of a condemnation award allocable to its furniture, fixtures, loss of good will, and moving expenses.

11. The tenant's right to self-insure.
12. Rights of offset for the landlord's defaults including its failure to pay the allowance.
13. Arbitration of disputes.
14. The landlord's responsibility for the tenant's broker's compensation.
15. A non-disturbance agreement from the landlord's lender.
16. A general requirement of reasonableness, promptness, and good faith when consents are required.
17. The use of the tenant's lease form.

Chapter 16
COMMON INTEREST OWNERSHIP
Rebecca Fischer

§ 16.02 THE DECLARATION

[B] Essential Terms

Page 1004, add to note 29:

In one case in Massachusetts, the tax assessor sought to assess, not the condominium project's common area, but instead, the rights to build additional units on that common area. The developer had specifically reserved those development rights in the project documents, and those rights had passed to the owners by operation of law. *See* § **16.10,** main volume and supplement, for a discussion of development rights. Applying Massachusetts statutes that prohibit the separate taxation of condominium common areas, the court rejected the assessor's attempt to sever the development rights from the underlying fee, and to subject the rights to separate taxation. *First Main Street Corp. v. Board of Assessors of Action,* 725 N.E.2d 1076 (Mass. App. Ct. 2000).

In addition, in Colorado, state law (based on UCIOA) prohibits a county tax assessor from taxing common areas as separate property. However, that law does not prevent the county from assessing certain parts of the common areas at separate rates. In *Manor Vail Condominium Ass'n v. Board of Equalization of Eagle County,* 956 P.2d 654 (Colo. Ct. App. 1998), the court confirmed the authority of the county tax assessor to assess certain common elements in a residential complex at a higher rate applicable to commercial properties. The common areas in question included a restaurant and meeting rooms that were open to the general public, and that were not claimed as being integral to the residential use of the individual condominium units.

§ 16.04 THE OWNERS ASSOCIATION—GENERAL POWERS AND DUTIES

[D] Power to Make Rules

Page 1027, add to note 62:

The decision in *Mulligan v. Panther Valley Property Owners Ass'n*, 766 A.2d 1186 (N.J. Super. Ct. App. Div. 2001), highlights several points in the debate on rules pitting the rights of the individual against the desires of the common interest community. In the wake of New Jersey's passage of "Megan's Law" (requiring that persons convicted of sex offenses register their names and addresses in public records), the members of the Panther Valley Property Owners Association adopted an amendment to their project declaration and their association bylaws, prohibiting any individual registered as a "Tier 3" offender under Megan's Law (the classification assigned to a person considered at highest risk of committing repeat offenses) from residing in the Panther Valley community. Although the appellate court refused to rule on a homeowner's challenge to the Megan's Law rule (for want of a sufficient record in the trial court), the court did not refrain from discussing the merits of the arguments. First, the court decided that a judicial review of a New Jersey community association's rule should be based on a "reasonableness" standard (in contrast to a less stringent "business judgment rule" standard). In making that determination, the court noted that the rule in dispute surfaced in an amendment to the community's governing documents, as opposed to the original project documents in place when the plaintiff owner bought her Panther Valley residence. For that reason, the court viewed the new rule as *not* entitled to the strong presumption of validity sometimes accorded restrictive covenants in place at the beginning of the project. Further justifying the reasonableness standard in reviewing the rule, the court noted that the amendment was passed (in accordance with the governing documents) by a simple majority vote, and not with substantial majority approval, which the court considered a more widely accepted procedure in community association practice.

Turning to the homeowner plaintiff's specific complaints, the court quickly dismissed arguments that the Megan's Law rule infringed on the owner's right to alienate her property. The effect of the rule was equal against all owners in the project, and the effect was also apparently insignificant, in light of the very small number of individuals disqualified from purchasing in the project because of the rule. However, the court worried more about the public policy implications of such a rule, if communities across the state were to adopt comparable versions and make housing inaccessible to Tier 3 registrants.

§ 16.07 DESIGN REVIEW

Page 1035, add to note 76:

In *Pagosa Lakes Property Owners Ass'n, Inc. v. Caywood*, 973 P.2d 698 (Colo. App. 1998), the association had sought a mandatory injunction requiring the removal of a manufactured home from an owner's lot. The manufactured home did not comply with the Uniform Building Code, in violation of standards set forth in unrecorded rules adopted by the board of directors after the defendant owners had purchased their lot. The subdivision predated Colorado's adoption of the Common Interest Ownership Act ("CIOA," the state's version of UCIOA), but among the CIOA sections that apply retroactively to pre-CIOA subdivisions are provisions that authorize an association to adopt and amend rules and regulations. The defendants argued that the association exceeded its authority in adopting and enforcing unrecorded restrictions on the property, but the court upheld the injunction. The court reasoned that the project declaration, which was recorded for the subdivision before the defendants' lot purchase, created broad powers in the association and the project's architectural review committee, and the purchasers were charged with notice of those powers and also with notice of the provisions of CIOA that governed the subdivision retroactively. Accordingly, the court declined to hold that the requirement for compliance with the Uniform Building Code could not be enforced unless the requirement was separately recorded in the public records.

§ 16.08 ASSESSMENTS BY THE ASSOCIATION

Page 1045, add to note 88:

The decision in *Linden Condominium Ass'n, Inc. v. McKenna*, 726 A.2d 502 (Conn. 1999), illustrates the importance of an association's timely collection of delinquent assessments, to avoid loss of dues more than six months in arrears. The Connecticut Supreme Court, interpreting state law modeled on UCIOA, held that a condominium association could not seek a deficiency judgment as part of its foreclosure action enforcing its priority lien for six months' amount of assessments, where the first mortgage redeemed the foreclosed unit by paying the association's priority claim.

§ 16.10   COMMERCIAL REAL ESTATE TRANSACTIONS

However, the court did permit the association to bring a wholly separate suit to recover the remaining assessment charges owed to the association.

Page 1045, add to note 89:

See Longanecker v. Diamondhead Country Club, 760 So. 2d 764 (Miss. 2000). The project covenants that required all assessments to be applied to each lot on an *equal* basis did not prevent the association from imposing different rates of assessments for security services on an *equitable* basis, depending on whether the lots in question were improved or unimproved.

§ 16.10   RIGHTS OF THE DECLARANT

Page 1066, add to note 102:

The decision, *Arrowhead by the Lake Ass'n, Inc. v. Arrowhead by the Lake, Inc.,* 2000 WL 33124430 (Conn. Super. 2000), details exactly what a condominium developer should not attempt in a last ditch, unilateral modification of the project documents. One day before the expiration of the developer control period contemplated under the original declaration, the developer recorded an amended declaration that purported to extend and expand the developer's right to build out the property, change the unit boundaries, and lower the voting approval requirements for changes to the use restrictions governing the units. The court issued a permanent injunction against the developer's implementation of the amendment, together with a decree vesting title in the condominium property in the unit owners, free and clear of the declarant's development rights.

Page 1069, add to note 120:

In jurisdictions without the statutory limitations imposed by UCIOA or the Uniform Condominium Act on the rights of the developer to direct the project association by making appointments to the board, courts may still restrict the developer's control to the start-up phases crucial to the development and marketing of the project. *See Unrau v. Kidron Bethel Retirement Servs., Inc.,* 27 P.3d 1 (Kan. 2001).

Page 1070, add to note 123:

The consequences of ignoring these guidelines were the subject of *Chesus v. Watts,* 967 S.W.2d 97 (Mo. Ct. App. 1998). The court used principles drawn from the state's Uniform Condominium Act and contract law to address claims of lot purchasers in a planned unit development. The court applied the doctrine of promissory estoppel to hold that the association had standing to sue the developer for the developer's failure to complete and deliver to the association the common area improvements that the developer had promised in return for the premium prices paid by the subdivision buyers.

§ 16.12 ENFORCEMENT OF THE DECLARATION

Page 1084, add to note 141:

A Pennsylvania case presented one court with an opportunity to confirm the power and validity of an attorneys' fees clause in a project declaration, when a homeowner who resisted a $1,200 assessment wound up paying the assessment and, in addition, more than $46,000 for attorneys' fees spent by the association in collecting the delinquent payment. *Mountain View Condominium Ass'n v. Bomersbach*, 734 A.2d 468 (Pa. Commw. Ct. 1999). The homeowner's case was not helped by the facts that the initial tally of attorneys' fees sought by the association with the first demand for payment was only $500, and that the docket in the case revealed a homeowner defendant "who engaged in trench warfare" in fighting the assessment. *See also Bitting v. Central Pointe Condominium Bd. of Managers*, 970 S.W.2d 898 (Mo. Ct. App. 1998).

Page 1085, add to note 143:

In *Ferrary v. Behan*, 25 Conn. L. Rptr. 408 (Conn. Super. Ct. 2001), a real estate agency and real estate broker were allowed to enforce Connecticut's version of the UCIOA. The plaintiffs were not owners, but instead, agents for owners in the project. The brokers won damages for commissions lost when sales of condominium units in the project, listed by the plaintiffs, were derailed by the project association's failure to deliver to the prospective purchasers the disclosures in the form of a resale certificate required by the state's Act. As the brokers fit the definition of persons adversely affected by the association's noncompliance with the Act, they were entitled to remedies under the Act.

CHAPTER 17
BANKRUPTCY
James R. Stillman

§ 17.01 AN INTRODUCTION TO BANKRUPTCY COUNSELING

[C] The Eclectic Sources of Bankruptcy

Page 1103, add after carryover sentence at top of page:

The authorized number of bankruptcy courts in the United States is found in 28 U.S.C. § 152(a)(2).

[D] What Happens to the Other Side When a Bankruptcy Case Is Commenced?

Page 1103, add to note 4:

28 U.S.C. § 152(a)(1) has been revised to provide for 14-year terms for bankruptcy judges.

Page 1104, add to note 7:

The automatic stay even prevents *enforcing* a claim against the debtor that the bankruptcy court itself awarded during the bankruptcy case. *See Temecula v. LPM Corp. (In re LPM Corp.)*, 269 B.R. 217 (B.A.P. 9th Cir. 2001).

Page 1106, replace note 24:

   [24] 11 U.S.C. §§ 363(f) (power of bankruptcy court to sell free of liens); 361(e) (right of creditor to demand adequate protection).

Page 1107, add to note 30:

   Notwithstanding *LaSalle*, bankruptcy lawyers have proven relentless and creative in trying to formulate real estate plans under which the exist-

§ 17.02[A] COMMERCIAL REAL ESTATE TRANSACTIONS

ing owners keep control. *See, e.g., Beal Bank, S.S.B. v. Waters Edge Ltd. Partnership*, 248 B.R. 668 (D. Mass. 2000).

§ 17.02 THE PURCHASE AND SALE AGREEMENT

[A] Counseling the Purchaser Regarding Bankruptcy

[3] Risk to Purchaser's Investments in Improvements

Page 1111, add at end of second bullet:

The escrow agreement itself is an executory contract that the debtor can almost always break. *See generally* Byrne, "Escrows and Bankruptcy," 48 Bus. Law. 761 (1993).

[8] When the Seller Is the Master Developer

Page 1114, note 41, correct citation for **Garfinkel** *article:*

28 Real Prop. Prob. & Tr. J. 82 (1993).

[B] Counseling the Seller Regarding the Risks Associated With a Buyer's Bankruptcy

[2] How Sellers Try to Draft "Exceptions" to Assignability

Page 1116, add to third paragraph:

Experienced practitioners expect that any clause in a commercial real estate contract that purports to require performance solely by an existing party will be attacked under 11 U.S.C. § 365(e)(1), which nullifies so-called *ipso facto* clauses in bankruptcy. *See, e.g., Crow Dev. Ltd. Partnership v. Jamboree LLC (In re Crow Winthrop Operating Partnership)*, 241 F.3d 1121 (9th Cir. 2001) ("change of ownership" prohibition rendered ineffective).

[4] No Automatic Way to Terminate Contract Once Bankruptcy Intervenes

Page 1117, add to second paragraph:

An automatic price escalation clause was found to be "bankruptcy neutral" and therefore enforceable against the debtor in *Yates Dev. Inc. v. Old*

BANKRUPTCY § 17.06[B]

Kings Interchange, Inc. (In re Yates Development Inc.), 256 F.3d 1285 (11th Cir. 2001).

§ 17.06 THE LEASE

[A] Bankruptcy Checklist for Representing the Tenant

Page 1130, add new bullet at end of subsection [A]:

- The tenant has a very strong position should the debtor/landlord have assumed the lease formally during the case, then elect to breach. This happens most commonly when a liquidation trustee is appointed after the reorganization effort fails. *See, e.g., Einstein/Noah Bagel Corp. v. Smith (In re BCE West, L.P.)*, 264 B.R. 578 (B.A.P. 9th Cir. 2001) (discussing the scope of the "administrative claim" such a tenant enjoys in the case).

[B] Bankruptcy Checklist for Representing the Owner/Lessor

Page 1130, add to text after note 66:

But insofar as the automatic stay will not toll the mere running out of time, where state law provided for a truly self-executing lease termination effective some number of days after the service of a notice of termination, and the notice was served pre-petition, then all rights of the debtor in the premises were extinguished and the lease could not be administered in bankruptcy, even when the period ran out after the case was commenced. *Policy Realty Corp. v. Treber Realty LLC*, 2000 WL 534265 (2d Cir. May 2, 2000) (New York law; unpublished opinion); and *see* note 81 main volume, and accompanying text.

Page 1130, add after note 66:

- This includes any right to spend or apply the security deposit, insofar as the deposit consists of money or other property posted by the tenant. In bankruptcy law, the landlord's rights in the security deposit will be deemed a *security interest in* "property of the estate," and therefore the automatic stay will apply. *See United States v. Whiting Pools, Inc.*, 462 U.S. 198, 207 (1983).

- In most cases, the bankruptcy filing will not prevent the landlord from suing third-party lease guarantors or from having access to other third-party credit enhancement instruments, such as letters of credit, because third parties are generally not protected by the automatic stay in the tenant's case. *See, e.g., Kopolow v. P.M. Holding Corp. (In re Modern Textile, Inc.)*, 900 F.2d 1184 (8th Cir. 1990); *In re Page*, 18 B.R. 713 (D.D.C. 1982) (rejecting contrary aberrant analysis of *In re Twist Cap, Inc.*, 1 B.R. 284 (Bankr. M.D. Fla. 1979)); *Arden v. Hotel Partners (In re Arden)*, 176 F.3d 1226 (9th Cir. 1999). Is a landlord therefore better off, from the bankruptcy point of view, to take a letter of credit and *not* cash for the security deposit? At least one commentator thinks so, Anton N. Natsis, "When Lease Is More," 23 L.A. Law. 46, 48–49 (No. 10 Jan. 2001), while the traditional advice is for the landlord to take cash, as much as can be gotten, *see, e.g.,* Misha D. Weidman, "Negotiating Commercial Leases," CEB Action Guide 38 (Spring 1993).

Other recent cases involving the landlord's access to third-party letters of credit (while the tenant is in bankruptcy) include *In re Farm Fresh Supermarkets of Maryland, Inc.*, 257 B.R. 770 (Bankr. D. Md. 2001); *In re Hechinger Investment Inc.*, 2001 Bankr. LEXIS 148 (D. Del. Jan. 29, 2001). The bankruptcy court enjoined the landlord from drawing on the letter of credit, where the tenant's only default under the lease was filing the bankruptcy case. *In re Metrobility Optical Sys., Inc.*, 268 B.R. 326 (Bankr. D.N.H. 2001).

Page 1131, add to note 71:

The landlord's reasonable attorneys' fees will also be included in the cure price, in most cases. *See In re Crown Books Corp*, 269 B.R. 12 (Bankr. D. Del. 2001).

Page 1132, add to note 77:

Yet the trend in bankruptcy is decidedly against enforcement of lease recapture or profit-sharing clauses, however artfully drafted. *See South Coast Plaza v. Standor Jewelers West, Inc. (In re Standor Jewelers West, Inc.)*, 129 B.R. 200, 202 (B.A.P. 9th Cir. 1991) (enforcing an "allocation provision" in the lease would not be permitted because it would "adversely affect the ability of the [tenant] in its rehabilitation effort"); *see also,* for a thorough discussion

BANKRUPTCY § 17.07[B]

with all the current citations, *In re Boo.Com North America Inc.*, 2000 Bankr. LEXIS 1559 (Bankr. S.D.N.Y. Dec. 15, 2000) (not for publication).

Page 1133, add to note 79:

Centerpoint Properties v. Montgomery Ward Holding Co. (In re Montgomery Ward Holding Corp.), 268 F.3d 205 (3d Cir. 2001) (rejecting proration approach; obligation to pay rent arises for purposes of 11 U.S.C. § 365(d)(3), when the duty to perform arises under the terms of the lease).

Page 1133, add to text after note 80:

Unless the debtor formally rejects the lease in bankruptcy, the debtor's obligation to pay rent post-petition on a lease of commercial real property may continue even where the debtor surrendered possession before commencing bankruptcy. This happens when the landlord "accepted the keys" but expressly did not intend to terminate the lease (consistent with an election regarding remedies). *See, e.g., In re CHS Electronics, Inc.*, 265 B.R. 339 (Bankr. S.D. Fla. 2001).

[C] Synthetic Leases and Other Financing Leases

Page 1134, add to note 84:

See also In re Greenfield Dry Cleaning & Laundry, Inc., 249 B.R. 634 (Bankr. E.D. Pa. 2000) (a settlement agreement in which the lease was continued for some period of time was styled as a "license" and therefore cost the landlord its priority right to rent payments).

§ 17.07 THE REAL ESTATE SECURED LOAN

[B] Commonly Asked Questions About Loan Documents in Bankruptcy

Page 1138, add to note 95:

The correct view, even in a "title theory jurisdiction," is that the rental assignment creates only a lien. *See Cavros v. Fleet Nat'l Bank (In re Cavros)*, 262 B.R. 206 (Bankr. D. Conn. 2001).

Page 1139, add to note 98:

In addition, a non-consensual sale pre-confirmation, *i.e.*, during the pendency of the bankruptcy case, is not uncommon. *See* 11 U.S.C. § 363(f)(3) (sale by bankruptcy court of property allowed where objecting party holds only a lien).

Page 1140, add to note 103:

The need for the lender unequivocally to have *given notice* of its intent to collect default rate interest, in order to have a claim for default rate interest in bankruptcy, was the subject of *Beal Bank v. Crystal Properties (In re Crystal Properties)*, 268 F.3d 743 (9th Cir. 2001).

Page 1141, add to note 108:

A yield-maintenance fee was recently disallowed by the bankruptcy court in *In re Schwegmann Giant Supermarkets Partnership*, 264 B.R. 823 (Bankr. E.D. La. 2001).

Page 1142, add to note 111:

So, for example, a statutory right to attorneys' fees equal to 15 percent of the loan principal under Georgia law was not allowed in bankruptcy as part of the secured claims. *Royal v. Welzel (In re Welzel)*, 260 F.3d 1284, *mod. on rehearing* en blanc, 275 F.3d 1308 (11th Cir. 2001).

INDEX

References are to sections.

Design/build
    advantages, 4.09[C]
    disadvantages, 4.09[D]
    growth of design/build, 4.09[A]
    history, 4.09[B]
    making it work, 4.09[G]
    ramifications of selection, 4.09[F]
    selecting the right project delivery system, 4.09[E]

Environmental risk insurance
    brownfield insurance, 11.12[D]
    cost overrun insurance, 11.12[C]
    policy exclusions, 11.12[F]
    pollution legal liability insurance, 11.12[B]
    secured creditor insurance, 11.12[E]
    types of coverage, 11.12[A]

Industrial leases
    condemnation and casualty provision, 12.15, Form 12-24

Loan documents
    lock-in and prepayment penalty clauses, 8.03[B][4]
    promissory note, 8.03[B]

Opinion letters
    sample legal opinion, App. 9C

Promissory note
    lock-in clauses, 8.03[B][4]
    prepayment penalty clause, 8.03[B][4]

Risk allocation and insurance
    deed of trust insurance, indemnity, and waiver provisions, App. 10G